C000144130

Cumbria
The War Years

Lake District Life during the 1940s

∾

JUNE THISTLETHWAITE

Thyme Press

Cumbria The War Years

Cover photograph by Keith Bales Photography, Workington

Published by Thyme Press, 5 Finley Close,
Kendal, Cumbria LA9 6DW

First Published 1997

Typeset by Indent Ltd, Kendal
Printed by Kent Valley Colour Printers Ltd, Kendal

British Library Cataloguing in Publication Data
A Catalogue record for this book is available from the British Library
ISBN 0 9531695 1 0

Contents

Acknowledgements

I am grateful to all interviewees for their patience and time so freely given. To Mr J Grisenthwaite (County Archivist), Mr G Rothery (Workington), Mr T Furnass (Kendal), Employees of Ryders PLC (Kendal) who provided valuable advice. Shambles Antiques (Kendal) for loaning some of the items used for the front cover of this book.

Most of the photographs in the book are produced courtesy of the interviewees. I am grateful for the loan of photographs from Mrs H Bracken (page 22), Mr J Becker (Carlisle) (photograph on page 69), Whitehaven News (photograph on page 151), Mr D Garner, Curator of the Cumbria Police Museum (Penrith) (photographs on p.132), the Librarian at Sedbergh School (photograph on page 20), Mr J Nixon at the RAF Museum, Millom (Haverigg) (photographs on p.150 & 151); British Steel PLC (Cumbria) (photograph on page 91), North West Evening Mail at Barrow-in-Furness (photographs on p. 11, 52, 53 & 149; photocopy page 48, 59), the West Cumberland Times and Star at Workington (photocopies on pages 14, 78, 89, 93, 94, 108, 173, 174; photographs on pages 127& 161), Cumberland and Westmorland Herald at Penrith (photocopies on pages 25, 65, 76, 79, 81, 110, 111, 118, 120, 121, 137) Westmorland Gazette at Kendal (photocopies on pages 18, 32, 67, 70, 71, 72, 73, 136, 145, 156, 157, 164, 180 photographs on p.98, 134 & 142) Cumbrian Newspapers Ltd at Carlisle, (photocopy on page 58, 79; photograph p.103); the Beacon Heritage Centre at Whitehaven (photographs on pages 63 & 64); the Railway Museum at York (photocopy on p.143).

I am indebted to the editors of the above newspapers and the corresponding local libraries for giving me permission to use the photocopies of articles and adverts taken from the war-time editions of their newspapers; the University College St Martin's at Ambleside and Kendal Archives both kindly allowed me to photocopy material (pages 41, 114, 129, 138, 144, 178) also the National Dairy Council forwarded to me material (pages 23, 45, 112, 179) To all the above, many grateful thanks.

Every effort has been made to contact the copyright holders and I apologise most sincerely if I have failed to acknowledge anyone and would be grateful of being notified of any corrections to be incorporated in any future editions.

Cumbria

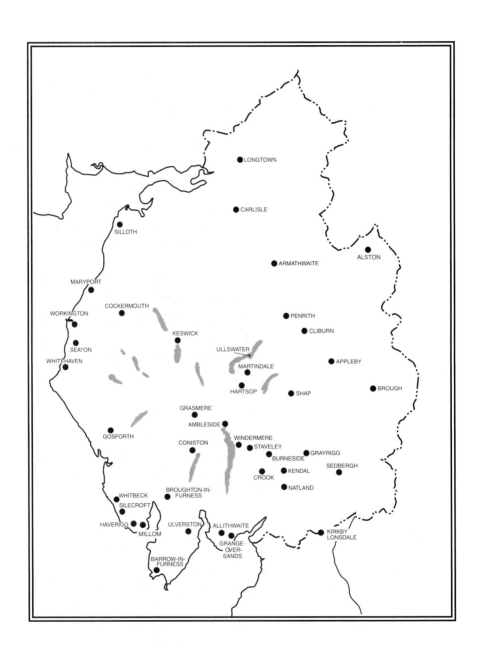

Introduction

In the introduction to my book 'Cumbrian Women Remember', I wrote of the ladies interviewed, that '...the war years were taken in their stride. Yes, there were bombings, yes it was frightening. It was acknowledged as a difficult time ... and that was that!

Most people who remember the war years are reluctant to speak about them. It isn't a fashionable subject and they're accused of living in the past. But what a past! Those years are mostly chronicled for the international part our country played; or life in the British cities, devastated by the bombing. Unfortunately, not quite as much is known about our county and its inhabitants during that time.

Paradoxically, 'our county' as we know it, didn't exist during the war years. The area we now call Cumbria consisted of Cumberland and Westmorland, with the addition of part of Lancashire to the south, and a slice of Yorkshire to the east. It is noticeable, that some interviewees speak of Cumbria, while others refer to Cumberland or Westmorland.

I didn't know much about the war years in this county. I knew there'd been bombing Barrow-in-Furness, barbed-wire along the coast and I can vaguely remember rationing and having to queue for sweets. That was the sum total of my knowledge. So it seemed like a good idea to record people's recollections of that time.

When one of my sons notices my tape recorder surfacing, he announces, 'Mother's going out accosting old people, again'. Accost, yes, but old people? No Way. It was a very moving experience listening to these stories being told. As I spoke to interviewees, and as they hesitantly started answering my questions, memories came flooding back to them. And before me sat a young man or woman. They spoke as teenagers do, with the same definite opinions and almost gleeful disregard for convention.

Eileen, remembering her place of work, stated emphatically, "My aim was getting out of there. When I finished work, I was off." Joe at Docker, his favourite expression for old men in authority (but younger than he is today) was, "Dothering old buggers." George at Kendal recalled the Riot Act being read out to him and other young soldiers more than once because of their behaviour. John at Salterbeck remembered nicking coal and ammunition. Oh dear, definitely not what I was expecting to hear from senior citizens but much more interesting and entertaining.

Among the men who worked on the land, there was pathos that they 'only worked on a farm.' Young as they were, at the outbreak of war, they wanted to join up. That was not to be. They were of much more importantance helping to plough, harvest and look after the cattle. But it hurt very much. There was heartbreak for Eleanor when her son's ship was torpedoed. The hurt for John at Barrow when his brother's plane was shot down, just days before the ending of the war.

Whatever anyone's story was about, to me they were fascinating. Each one so different with pathos or humour. I am only sorry there are still many tales left untold. Hopefully, before too long, I'll hear a voice saying, "Mother's going out accosting old people, again!"

ONE

'Margaret, they're all OURS!!'

cx

***Ethel Smith**, born 1926 on The Marsh, Workington.*

I was still at Newlands Girls School at Workington when the war started. The thing I can remember about school was, we had taken French for two years and all of a sudden these lessons were dropped. Teachers from all schools were being called away to go to war. The ones left behind filled in, often at the expense of their own subjects.

Newlands Girls School 1939
Back row l to r: Ethel Smith (nee Fisher); Margaret Elwin;
Valery Fisher. Front row l to r: Irene Hodgson;
Olga Fitzsimmons; Evelyn (?)

At about that time, Woolworths sent word to our school, asking if girls would like to work in their store on a Saturday. That was to see if they would like a job there when they were old enough to leave school a few months later. So I worked at Woolworths on a Saturday and eventually went full-time when I left school at the end of the summer term.

I worked on the sweets and biscuits counter. Both sweets and biscuits were rationed and there were big queues to buy them. I don't know how people knew there was going to be biscuits in stock because I didn't even know and I worked on the counter. But people just joined a queue and sometimes didn't even know when they got to the end of it what they were queuing for.

One or two girls that I knocked around with were trying to move from one job to another. I suppose you moved if you could get more money. Well, a factory opened at Seaton, so a few of us went for an interview and managed to get a job there. We travelled by bus every day from Workington and the top section would be full of the gang I'd gone to school with.

A lot of people don't even know about the Eugene factory which made ladies perms at Seaton. Our job was to fold a sachet and paper together. Somehow or other, when they were folded together, it was rolled onto a person's head when they were having a perm. But you know, when you are fourteen of fifteen years old - well, only a kid really - and working away, you used to wonder, "Is this secret work?" With the war being on there wasn't many people we knew having perms and we definitely thought, "There's something fishy here." We really did wonder if it was genuine perms we were making or something secret.

I can only remember one occasion of bombing at Workington and the raid finished up at Silloth. People reckoned the planes were trying to bomb the Steel Works at Workington. But down at Barrow-in-Furness, there was devastation. I was down at my auntie and uncle's who had the Catholic Club at Barrow, when they were bombed out of there. This club was a huge building, right next to St Mary's Catholic Church. When the bombing started we had to run about four doors (houses) along the street and use their cellars as a shelter. I remember uncle Eddie grabbing the club's till and taking it to the cellar with him. But with the bomb blast he was thrown backwards, still holding the till.

Fortunately none of us were hurt but my auntie and uncle never got back to the club because of the bomb damage. They went to live at Askam for a while and finished up at Walney Island. Houses were just flattened with the blast from the land-mines and were never built up again. People reckoned that if all the mines had gone off in Barrow that were dropped, there wouldn't have been anything standing.

My brother, Danny, who was three years older than me was working at the Post Office as a telegram boy at Workington. There were three telegram boys and they covered the whole area on push-bikes. The hardest part for Danny was to take telegrams to people when their sons or husbands were killed or missing. But by the time he was twenty, he joined the Royal Corps

Bomb Damage at Barrow-in-Furness

of Signals. So with Danny going away, I thought "I want to go as well."

A few of us had now moved from the Eugene factory to the Cloth factory at Siddick, where we were making khaki cloth for the army. That was better money and I quite liked weaving. Noisy, but I still liked it. But two girls left the cloth factory and went into the Timber Corps at Wetherby, so I decided to try for that.

I filled the forms in and asked to go into the Timber Corps as I didn't really fancy farm work. Later I got word back, yes, I'd be given the choice of work but could I leave home as soon as I was seventeen because there were vacancies at a hostel up at Longtown.

I went by train up to Longtown and the hostel was in the centre of the town. It was an L-shaped building, divided into parts for where you ate, slept and had showers and baths. There were about thirty bunks, which were very hard. I think our wage was about twenty-six shillings a week and out of that we had to pay for our board. So I never really had enough money to send home.

For my first job I went with Daisy, a girl from London, to the last farm in England called English Town. I thought maybe I'd be doing some hedging but no, there was no mention of that. It was harvest time and I was given a horse and cart to lead. Well, I'd never been near a horse before and it stepped on my foot. Fortunately there wasn't much damage done because we wore quite heavy shoes for working in.

Once in the field, it was "get up there", as if you'd know how to do all these things. Here was me on top of the cart and the sheaves of corn were forked up to me. I had to stack them so they wouldn't fall off the cart. Well, I'd never been on the top of a cart in my life. But I couldn't say that I didn't enjoy the work, because I did. I finished up working at that farm for three weeks during the harvest and didn't want to move.

Land Army girls having a well-deserved rest
Ethel is left, on the back row.

It was a very good farm and the farmer and his wife, Mr and Mrs Taylor were very kind and generous. You were given a ten o'clock and a three o'clock (snack) and a meal at lunch-time. Farmers weren't forced to give you a meal, as we each had a box of food from the hostel. That box was rubbish. Sandwiches were put straight into a big tin box. They didn't even put a piece of paper round the sandwiches and wrap them up. I never ate any of the food as it was atrocious. So I didn't open my box, and hoped that somebody would give me a three o'clock at the farm I was working at.

I was on lots and lots of farms at Longtown. After you'd done your jobs on one farm, they wanted somebody at another one and you were moved there. Oddly enough I was with my friend Margaret and we were sent up near to Ecclefechan. Now, that's in Scotland and the Scots had their own Land Army. But anyhow, we were sent up to this place and the farmer gave us a horse and cart and told us to go and pick some stones from a field. So Margaret and me set off and the hill we went down was nearly vertical. Of course you felt that the horse was going to land on your back.

We worked away in the field, time marched on and we set off back to the farm. Going up the hill, I said to Margaret, "What's happening?" The sky was absolutely full of parachutists. We actually thought we were being invaded but it was our own troops practising. By the time we got back to the farm yard, all the parachutists were there and having a cup of tea. There was dozens and dozens of them and here lands two seventeen year olds', walking among all these fellas. I turned to Margaret and said, "Margaret, they're all OURS!!"

Longtown was brilliant. There was hundreds of troops and that's why it was brilliant. There were army camps nearby and the aerodrome (RAF Longtown). Some of the pilots were learning in Tiger Moths. If we were doing hedging or working in a field, they almost hit us, they were so low. They used to hedge-hop and I've seen the pilots crash onto the ground and get out and walk away.

Being Land Girls, you used to get invitations from all over the place. The invitations used to come to the hostel, not to an individual person but to the lady who looked after us. The warden was quite a glamorous lady, very smart and about fifty years old. Us girls had to be in the hostel by ten o'clock during the week. On a Saturday night, we could have a late pass for eleven o'clock from the warden.

But there wasn't any question of coming back to the hostel and saying, "I'm sorry that I'm five minutes late. It didn't work. You'd probably get stopped from going out for one night. Occasionally, on a Saturday night, we were allowed to go and stay at the YWCA at Carlisle. From there, we'd go to the Cameo Dance Hall, which had the 'big band' sounds.

We were allowed dances in our hostel and the warden used to put on a buffet for us. Two of the girls were wonderful pianists, so we always had music and a nice hall for dancing. I've always liked dancing and jiving. Most of the lads that I danced with were Scottish, because in my opinion, they were the best dancers of the lot.

I was only seventeen at this time and I remember my friend Kay telling me about her niece. This niece was at New Brighton and getting invited to all these socials on board ship with the Navy and having a whale of a time. I didn't blame her. You see, I don't think there was any fear like there is now about going anywhere. Anybody you met, you thought they were all right. That's how I went through life, finding they were all right. It was a different kind of world. We were a lot more caring and friendly during the war years.

Every now and again, the Land Army used to split the girls up and send them to different hostels. I used to think that was a silly thing to do because you'd all made friends. Still, I didn't feel too unhappy when I was moved to Silloth. Our hostel there, Causeway Head, had been a vicarage and had no electricity so we had oil lamps.

There was a large aerodrome at Silloth, with Coastal Command and RAF personnel (No 22 Unit and No 1 Coastal Operations Training Unit.) So again, we got loads of invitations to socials and there was a dance hall in the town. There was plenty to do and I was always OK because I just loved to dance. So long as there was a dance, it didn't matter to me where we were.

There was one market garden at Wigtown we went to work at. We were sent to do some weeding and when we completed that, the chap said, "You can fill your lunch box with strawberries." That's the only time I can remember anybody saying you could have anything. Of course, some of the girls tried to send the strawberries home to their mothers. But my mam used to say, "Don't worry about me as long as you get something to eat, yourself."

I'll tell you something else. I didn't like margarine. I couldn't eat it because it made me ill. So my mam used to send me her butter ration. And if

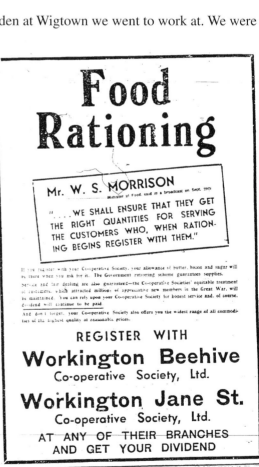

there was anybody near at hand who would sell her their butter coupon, my mam would trade or buy it for me. At Causeway Head, we got one square of butter on a Sunday and the rest of the time it was margarine. So I always looked forward to Sunday and my butter. I really did.

From Silloth we went to work at Aigle Gill farm, near Aspatria. When we got there, there were German prisoners-of-war working. If there were Germans around, we weren't supposed to work very near even though there were armed army lads with them. But there was no trouble with the Germans.

Anyway, at Aigle Gill the Germans were ditching and we were having our ten o'clock when the rain started. Now, when it rained, we were allowed to 'rain off', which meant stay at the farm until the weather cleared up. When we eventually went back to the field we'd been working in, the Germans had used straw to cover our coats and keep them dry. They'd also cut a turnip into a face and put straw round the top for hair. One coat was laid out with the turnip attached, to look like a land girl. Besides the coat was a note written in German.

The coat that the Germans had used belonged to our forewoman. She'd gone to school over in Germany before the war and was able to translate the note. They'd written, 'Hope everything is dry, land girls.' We thought it was rather amusing and at least we had dry coats. But our forewoman was a bit prejudiced as her boyfriend had been an RAF pilot and was shot down over Germany.

It was while we were at Aigle Gill that two of our girls each sent a puppy home to their mothers. The farm dog had pups so Kay sent one to Warrington and Esther sent one to Wigan. Well, their mothers didn't know anything about them being sheepdogs. By the time the dogs grew, Esther's poor mother used to go all round Wigan looking for the dog. It didn't want to be in the house, did it?

It's VJ night that I remember. There was a crew of Canadians over at Silloth at that time and five or six of us booked a taxi to the Stag Inn at Crosby. The Inn at that time was just like a house and they kept a barrel of beer in the kitchen. That didn't bother me as I was never a drinker and just had lemonade.

When we left the Land Army, it was a disgrace. We didn't get any money and were told we could go home in our shirt, shoes and overcoats but no trousers. Somebody said, "We'll look sick going home without trousers on, won't we?" Well, my brother Danny had sent me a camera and I took a photo of two of the girls standing without any trousers on.

I kept in touch with the land army girls after the war. Esther from Wigan used to come home with me when we had our week-end passes. For longer

*"We'll look sick going home without
any trousers on, won't we?"*

passes, I went to Wigan with Esther. Then after the war, my mam and dad used to follow the rugby matches and met her parents at Wigan and we've stayed friends ever since.

Looking back, I thought the war was never going to finish as we had been told it would be over in no time at all. It was an odd time. People were so friendly but I never thought I'd be working alongside German prisoners when we were still at war. But for the lads in the forces, it was different. With my first husband, Dick, it wasn't for a long, long time later that I realised why he didn't want to talk about Burma and such places. It was outrageous what they went through. Really, in Cumbria we weren't near enough to the war. It wasn't like it was in London or Coventry. I mean, in Workington, we didn't have anything, did we?

*Ethel was widowed twice, has two sons and is
Secretary of the Workington Camera Club.*

TWO

'The top brass couldn't keep his face straight'

∽

Ted Morphet, born 1921 at Sedbergh where he has farmed all his life.

1938 and '39 weren't bad years for farming and we were sort of recovering economically here in England. There was a bit of money stirring again and you could buy and sell. But in southern Ireland they hadn't recovered, and that's when a lot of these Irish lads came over here to the farms. They were coming over to help with the harvest and haytime and pick cabbage. We had Irish lads who'd been down south harvesting and come up here for a month's haytiming. Then they'd continue on to somewhere else to pick 'praties' as they said, before going back home to get their little harvest in. But they came back every year and mostly to the same farms all through the war years.

We didn't have any of these Irish lads on our farm but I worked with plenty on other farms and, by gum, they were glad of the money they made. They all said they were at starving point back in Ireland. Good workers they were, and good with a scythe on these steep fells round here. Yes, they had to be good workers because you worked nineteen hours and slept for five.

I went to a fell head spot (farm) myself every summer for a month during the war. One time I went and this chap had 'lost' his wife. His two kids had gone to an aunt at Tebay to be looked after, so we were on our own. I was on a pound a day and he sez, "Now, thou's gonna have to work to earn thy money as thou's getting more money than me." I had the scythe and he had the horses. Five o'clock every morning we started and he had a brown jug full of bacon fat with a knife stuck into it, a loaf of bread, and that was it. That's what we ate until we finished at midnight, then we had a fry-up of bacon and eggs. He made me earn my money, I'll tell you.

As soon as the war started, we had the War Ag (War Agricultural Executive) which was made up of local retired farmers, and they tried to tell us what to do. They were responsible for each area growing what it was told to grow. We all had our own allocation of potatoes to grow, otherwise we could grow what we liked. Actually, that was my main job in war time, going round ploughing, stitching and putting potatoes in. I travelled round with a couple of horses to farms where some folk were too old, some were too idle and some had no interest in potatoes. They were not arable men, you see. None of us were.

I remember going to one spot and I had to stitch this ground up, put muck into the stitches, plant the spuds and split the stitches. The day started all right. I had my own meals with me and the lady of the house and an old chap came and helped. The owner, he never came near me. I could see him sitting on this bridge watching me all day. I was brewing up (angry) by night as he hadn't turned up to help. Anyway, when I was pricking the stitches, I hit a big rock, which I lifted out of the ground with a stick. The stick came up and knocked my two front teeth out. Broke them straight off. By the time I'd finished and went into the yard, I doubled what I was going to charge him, moneywise. He just paid me what I'd asked for. I wished then I'd doubled the price up again.

The War Ag actually supplied men and tractors to plough and do whatever you wanted, but they made an awful mess of it. They used these Fordson tractors which were too big. You see, a lot of land round here has a bit of clay in it and these heavy tractors consolidated it. They also dug up a lot of the old stone drains that are just so far under the soil.

There was supposed to be restrictions on everything. We even had our own ration books for feeding our cattle, and it was a job getting plenty of food for them sometimes. We had to go and get on our knees at their (War Ag) office and beg. And at auction, calves and sheep were graded as to their price by the ministry. Such as calves, they were sold for five, ten, fifteen shillings or a pound, depending on their size.

We had our own hens, and eggs were sold locally on our milk round. A lot of people had hens supplied by breeders and hatchers at Preston. Folk were supplied with the chickens and they had to supply the firm with eggs. They were under contract to do this, and a very good thing it was. You were paid half as much again as you could sell your eggs locally. But we didn't have much trouble with foxes. They were great hunting men then, you know. Every farmer was a hunter and had a gun. Most moonlight nights we'd be out. There was patches of kale, and rabbits would come off the fell for a feed. So we'd circle the patch, put a terrier in and wait. A lot of rabbits supplied the rent at some homes.

We always bought pigs and used to feed them until they were that damned fat, they couldn't walk about. They were so fat it was unbelievable, but bacon was more fat than lean in those days. My stepfather was a butcher and he butched for two of the local butchers. We actually had a slaughterhouse here on the farm and we could strip the lard off a pig, roll it up to melt down for your cooking fat. Beautiful lard, it was.

Officially I don't think there was any evacuees here at Sedbergh. But unofficially we had some of my mother's relations from Liverpool come and stay with us as their nerves had gone with all the bombing. Then two boys also from Liverpool came and stayed with us, whose relations lived locally. These two young lads had been to a youth club in Liverpool and when they went home, their house wasn't there. Their mother and father had received a direct hit and no trace was ever found of them.

I think it'll be safe after all these years to tell you a story now. Armstrong Siddeley were building components for aeroplanes round here and that brought a lot of money into the valley. As well as local labour, men from outside were employed and were on good wages for working very long days. One bloke, a great boozer he was, said to me, "I want so many hams as I'm going back down to Coventry next week." Off he went round these farmhouses and saw all these hams hanging up. Beautiful stuff - it makes my mouth water now to think of them. Anyway, this chap tempted the folk with all the money he had, gathered these hams up and down Coventry with them.

There was a bit of black market then as where there's money, there's always somebody trying to do something, isn't there? One day a chap came to see me who wanted a certain number of heavy turkeys. All over twenty pounds in weight they had to be. Well, when he came for them, the turkeys were all up in the trees. That's where they perched at night to get out of't way of foxes. They weren't daft, you know. Well, that was great for us lads. We just threw stones to get these turkeys down and put them in sacks, as they were going live. A fiver each, that's what I got, which was a tremendous thing then as we'd never sold them for a pound before.

We had troops here during the war. They were stationed at Balliol on the Cautley Road. It was a rush job to get them houses. I helped on the building of that, for a shilling an hour, carting sand with a horse and cart. Little chalets were built with a concrete base and wooden cabins on top. The troops worked at Ingmire, which was a petrol dump. If that had gone up (caught fire) we'd have all gone up with it. Petrol in jerry cans was stored in Nissan huts for about a month or so. Then it was taken away and another batch arrived to be stored. So with all them troops, the pubs were alive.

There was the Pioneer Corps who were stationed at Castle Tower. That overlooks Sedbergh and was ideal for the Corps to report all aircraft that they saw. They would never be on the look-out on their own. There was always two of them round the clock. One Polish lad came down (crashed) behind Winder Fell and the only means of getting him down was by horse and sledge. The local police contacted me to go with them. You see, there wasn't any mountain rescue or ambulance then. It was a very steep part of the fell, even the horse couldn't manage it, so we went by foot for the last part and carried the body down to the bracken sledge.

Sedbergh School Cadet Corps, 1944

20

J.T.C.

The number of cadets undergoing training this term is 340. Of this number 105 possess Certificate A, including the 52 who passed in November.

A field day was held on 16th October. The senior platoons had exercises on fire control and fighting patrol in the Killington Bridge, Lincoln's Inn Bridge area. The ground was new and well suited to the lessons. The junior platoons together with the M.G. section had an exercise on concealment and patrols on Frostrow. The recruits had training in stalking under the observation of the Inteligence Section.

On November 21st, Col. S. J. Worsley, D.S.O., M.C., T.D., visited the contingent. Unfortunately it rained extremely hard and all the training had to be done indoors.

Major Collison and Captain Forster have both visited us this term and lectured either to the contingent or the Home Guard platoons. The latter have also had more training in night operations and automatic weapons.

Nine senior cadets attended the course at the Western Command Weapon Training School in the summer holidays, and it is hoped to send more cadets on other courses during the next holidays. The value of these courses, not only to the contingent but to the cadets themselves, is strongly emphasised by the War Office.

A.T.C.

Considerable progress has been made in every direction this term. A naval section has been formed which has been formed which practices semaphore and knotting, whilst the remainder, excepting the recruits, have been preparing to take the proficiency exam. About half term the flight was inspected and the inspection officer promised to make arrangements for the cadets to be "taken up," but so far these have failed to materialise. The uniforms have at last arrived as well as a large number of æronautical instruments, whilst progress in morse has been so rapid that every candidate for the proficiency exam. passed his test.

Sedbergh School Magazine 194?

In them early days, plane instruments wouldn't be what they are today and the pilots would run into mist on them fell tops. That Polish lad would have run straight into the fell and never have known what hit him. I know these fells but I still get lost in the mist. You can walk round in circles not knowing where you are. There was little bits of plane all over the spot. Later, folk from Catterick Camp came to take all the pieces of plane away, but they'd get very little of it. The rest had gone for souvenirs.

Home Guard duties were compulsory, of course. Although, saying that, one chap I knew wouldn't go and nobody could make him go. Anyway, we were very lucky as our meeting place was at the armoury at Sedbergh School, which had it's own junior cadet corps. When we joined the Home Guard, we started off with lumps of wood for rifles. So there we were marching about with lumps of wood. In charge of us was Lieutenant Colonel Downing, who had served in the First World War.

Once, the Home Guard was assembled for an inspection by the top brass. We were all immaculate with this top brass marching up and down the lines asking us questions. He stopped in front of this chap and said, "Now, Capstick, I want you to imagine you're in charge of the roadblock on the east side of Sedbergh. The Hun has landed at Hull and they're streaming across the country. What steps would you take, Capstick?" This fella looked at him and said, "Bloody big ones, Sir." The top brass couldn't keep his fact straight and just walked away.

The roadblocks that this top brass had mentioned, were on each of the five bridges coming into Sedbergh. That was our main job, manning these roadblocks. On each of these narrow bridges there was a concrete cylinder set into the ground. Horses and carts could pass over them but a tank couldn't. Our job was to look out for infiltrators. Like, if the Hun was riding on the horses and carts. But we never actually stopped anybody as we knew them all.

However, I had it cushy (easy) in the Home Guard. I had the only sten gun in the valley and was Downing's batman. So wherever he went, I went. When you think about it, if owt had happened and the Germans came to Sedbergh, they'd have already got most of England by the time they arrived here. It was a waste of time, really.

When the end of the war came, there was tables and chairs set out on every road and a beano going on. But rationing didn't just die, it went on for quite a long time. That affected the townspeople more than it did country folk. Then there was the winter of '47. Well, that was THE ONE, wasn't it? It was the worst winter we had in this valley. It came on 2 February and the snow came from the north-west. Everything was covered. There was lovely days but then the wind blew up at night and blew the snow back onto the roads we'd cleared. We worked for thirteen days trying to clear the roads. The local lads who were on the dole got five bob a week for doing that work. They had no choice, it was compulsory and some of them weren't fit to dig. They really weren't.

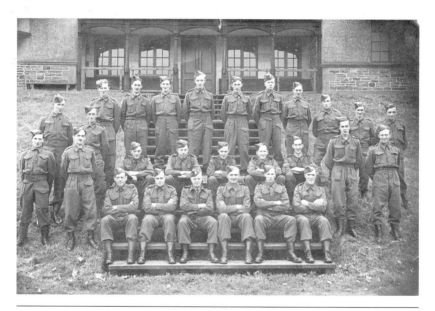

Sedbergh Home Guard outside the pavillion at Sedbergh School
Ted is standing fifth from the left, on the back row.

Region	Total Sales 000 Gallons		
	WINTER	SUMMER	YEAR
	Oct.1944 to Mar.1945	April to Sept.1944	Oct.1944 to Sept.1945
NORTHERN			
Cumberland	10,861	15,553	26,414
Durham	7,330	8,878	16,208
Northumberland	4,531	5,454	9,985
Westmorland	4,901	6,260	11,161
Yorks:East Riding	6,082	7,265	13,347
Yorks:North Riding	11,130	14,174	25,304

The biggest event after the war was the Milk Marketing Board taking our milk. You see, during the war, it was a struggle to get milk away to Leeds by train for those who were selling it. Then Mullin's, the lorry firm, started picking it up and taking it to the cheese factory at Appleby. However, the Milk Marketing Board guaranteed to take milk on a daily basis. And it didn't matter how little milk people had, it would still be picked up from their milkstand. I remember one chap who used to walk down the fields to his milk stand with a five-gallon can on his back. That was the easiest way of getting the milk down these steep fields. You see, being able to sell milk like this started people off. They got a little cheque. That was the first time they'd ever got cheques like that. They got themselves into business. That was the great thing for these Dales fellas, it was that.

Leader of the Young Farmers Club in the 1950s,
Ted a married man is now semi-retired.

THREE

'Everybody was pleased to see the breadman'

cx/

Sally Dixon, born at Netherton, near Maryport. Living at Cockermouth but working at Keswick when war was declared.

Sally C. 1940

In 1936 I went down to Dorking in Surrey to train as a children's nurse. But after a year I had to come home because, with being an only child, my mother was upset at me being so far away. I then started work as a manageress of Birkett's, the confectioners shop, at Station Road, Keswick.

To tell you the truth, when you're young, you just don't think about if there'll be a war. You're enjoying life and just don't want to be bothered about these things. I do remember the Sunday morning that war was declared, as it was announced over the radio. I'd been to church that morning and the news was also given out in church.

Gradually there was a big influx of people into Keswick. There was a Driving and Maintenance School at the Derwentwater Hotel. Roedean School from Brighton was at the Keswick Hotel, Newcastle High School took over the Queen's Hotel and St Catherine's College from Liverpool were evacuated to the Tower Hotel at Portinscale.

People queued for food at Birkett's shop and, although I started work at nine o'clock in the morning, it was sometimes nearly nine at night before I got cashed up and finished. People didn't have to register for bread and cakes at confectioners. You could get your bread but there wasn't the selection of bread that there is today. There was brown or white, either a small loaf or a large one which was called a pan loaf, teacakes and scones. We also had long buns with icing on top, called Sally Lunns, which sold well. Besides ordinary cakes such as vanilla slices and fruit tarts, you could still order a birthday cake, but it wasn't a fruit one like you get today, just a sponge cake. One on the best sellers was a round sponge cake with the top cut in half and lifted up with a meringue at each side. You won't remember them, but they were really special, with fresh cream inside.

Birkett's bakery was at Penrith, so I ordered each day for what had to go into the shop. Then the van from Penrith came in the morning, maybe at half past nine, unloaded our deliveries and then went off on his travels. The driver was a nice fella, and as I was just learning to drive at that time, I sometimes went with him to have a little drive. My half day off was on a Wednesday, so that would be the day I went with

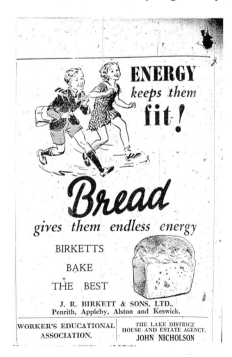

the driver, and he used to go as far as Embleton, round Cockermouth way and around the villages such as Borrowdale. I remember going to Borrowdale because there used to be flooding on the roads in winter. So everybody was pleased to see the breadman and you got a cup of tea wherever you went. Very nice, homely people they were in those villages.

I was still living at home and travelled each day from Cockermouth to Keswick. After we'd cashed up at night, many a time I was running to catch the ten-to-nine train home. I worked all day on a Saturday but the only reason I could work at Birkett's was because they didn't open on a Sunday. My father was against places being open on a Sunday.

Later on, I lived with a friend and her family at Keswick. As my parents had room at home, they had two evacuees living with them. One was a Welsh lad and the other was from down south. They were good company for my mam and she spoiled them, Oh, she ruined them. She used to bake for these two lads and make them all the things they liked. I remember I went home to Cockermouth one Sunday and she was seeing to what these two lads wanted, not about me. My mam really enjoyed having them and they kept in touch with her until she died.

I met my future husband, Bert, on Keswick railway station one night and we started to talk. He was in a group called Pushing Young People or P.U.P.s as it used to be called. So we started talking about this group and sort of got on with each other and started a courtship. It was different then because you had a proper courtship. We used to go for a walk, probably up Castle Head, and call at his married brother's for a cup of tea. Of course, I used to go to all sorts of things connected to P.UP.s with him. They did a lot for the town and held whist drives, dances, carnivals and all sorts. Bert was also in the Home Guard and they guarded Thirlmere Lake because the water pipes went down to Manchester. I think it was only one or two nights a week he went, but I know they used to enjoy themselves.

Bert was called up for the forces, so we got engaged in November 1941 and married the following February, in 1942, otherwise I'd have been called up. We married in Cockermouth on St Valentine's Day, and it was a very frosty, cold morning. We'd had snow and it was lying inches thick, so relatives coming to the wedding from Keswick had to get taxis. My bouquet didn't arrive and any flowers that could be had were made up into another bouquet for me.

Luckily my dad already had a pinstripe suit, and I used all his coupons as well as my own towards a wedding dress. In those days you had to have everything, a dress, wreath and veil, for a wedding. I bought all of those at Miss Chicken's shop in Cockermouth. Birkett's made me the wedding cake as a present. They'd also gave me a twenty-first birthday cake, too. So Mr

Courting days for Bert & Sally

and Mrs Birkett were very, very good to work for and I really enjoyed my time there.

Bert and I went to the Old England Hotel at Windermere for our honeymoon in a Wolsey car that belonged to his family. I remember that the wedding guests tied tin cans and all sorts to the back of the car and we stopped at the top of Dunmail Raise to take them all off. It was still bitterly cold with thirteen degrees of frost, and Windermere Lake was frozen over.

When my husband went back to his regiment I went to live with his mother in a seven-bedroomed house on the Penrith Road in Keswick. Bert had been the youngest of nine and the last one living with her, and I think it upset her terribly when he went away. So her daughter's girl, Mary went to live with 'Nanna' as we called her. I'd known Mary as she worked at the chemist's next door to Birkett's, and when I started courting with Bert, it was, "Oh, you're going with my Uncle Bert, aren't you?" So Mary and I, to this day, we're great friends and never had a cross word.

As Bert's family had the Keswick Steam Laundry I started work there after I married, doing the books. The laundry was the only one in Keswick and did the washing for all the hotels. There was thirty women working there and ten men, including two van men. The two big vans were on the road and covered Borrowdale, Braithwaite and Portinscale, collecting linen from the hotels. There was also some big houses in those days we'd collect from, such as Lady Rochdale's, Mrs Fowe's at Four Park and the Spedding family of Mirehouse who lived on the Bassenthwaite Road.

The laundry also did household washing for people and in those days there was a more personal service. We had ladies who ironed everything that was embroidered. It was all done properly and ironed on the wrong side, it wasn't just pushed through a colander. There were big colander machines but a lot of clothing was hand-ironed.

First of all, clothing was checked in by hand. Each item had initials put on in laundry ink. Maybe the mark was on the hem of some clothing or on the underside of a tablecloth. Then the laundry went through the different departments. One storey of the building had the washing machines and one person pushing sheets through the big colander and other person folding them at the other end. Later a folder was added to the colander, and that used to fold washing automatically. Items that needed to be ironed and packed, went to the department upstairs.

At the laundry we had to take in the washing from the schools and colleges who were evacuated here, as well as the soldiers' washing. So we had plenty of work to do. Students at Roedean School wore what were called 'jibbets'. These were like a blouse top of pure silk and they were lovely colours. I'm not sure if each class wore a different colour but they really did have beautiful clothes.

You see, a time was set aside for Rodean and other school's washing at the end of the week. Then, at the beginning of the week, all the soldiers' clothes came to be washed. Happy times. The lassies at the laundry used to have a good time with the soldiers from this Driving and Maintenance School. When their laundry was brought in the soldiers used to leave messages among it all for the girls, who used to enjoy that. In fact, two of the girls got married to D & M blokes. There wasn't an awful lot of tourist trade then, because people couldn't go on holiday through the war, like they do now. So really, all the laundry from the schools and army kept us all going.

Bert was with a London regiment, and at first had to go down south. So a lot of our courting, and the first part of married life, was done by letters. We wrote to each other every day, but sometimes you didn't get a letter each day, then three or four letters would arrive together. For a while I travelled to see Bert when I could get time off work to see him, even if it was just a weekend. I went to Saltcoates in Scotland, Ramsgate on two occasions, Brackley, Hinkley and Oxford. At some of these towns, such as

Oxford and Ramsgate, you had to have a permit to go to them because of the shelling and such like. So Bert would apply for a permit and send it to me. I used to travel by train from Keswick and these trains were always full of soldiers. Often you had to stand all the way as you couldn't get a seat. You couldn't go to the dining car for a meal, all that had finished. You had to take your own sandwiches on the journey or do without.

Bert always used to book me in somewhere nice when I was with him and I got to know the other soldiers he was with. He was in the artillery regiment and with a nice lot of blokes. At one time they were sent up to Scotland and given some embarkation leave. But Bert was put with another regiment, a Canadian lot, while his original regiment was sent to the Falkland Islands. After a while, I couldn't go and see Bert or have any contact with him at all. Later I found out that they were preparing for the D-Day landings. After that I didn't see him for sixteen months as he went through Holland, Belgium and then into Germany.

I suppose we must have celebrated when the war finished. But you see, our men were still away and you couldn't really celebrate when they were still away. The funny thing about all this was, just after the war, before Bert was demobbed, my niece and I went to Ambleside one afternoon. We were standing by the lakeside, when a boat with some soldiers on came to the landing stage. I recognised one soldier and it was the original regiment my husband had been with. They'd gone to the Falklands and were sent to Grasmere, of all places, before they were demobbed.

The war in Europe finished in May '45 and Bert came to Carlisle the following January and was demobbed from there. Then Bert started up on his own with a dry-cleaning business. He got a dry-cleaning machine and sent two girls to Penrith to train how to use it. Grand lassies they were, and one is still dry-cleaning.

After the war, hotels started up again and the tourist trade started to come in. Then came linen hire, so people weren't buying sheets to send to the laundry. After than came nylon sheets and folk could wash those themselves. In about 1970 our launderette was taken over but we were told that I could still have my laundry done free of charge and that continued for twenty years. In all those years, I'd never done any washing, thanks to the Keswick Steam Laundry. So when I look back, there's been some sad times but I've had a lot of nice things happen to me. I've had a lovely life, and the tourist trade, I think it's the tops. It keeps us going, doesn't it?

Sally, a widow with a family, is
President of Abbeyfield (Keswick) Society Ltd.

FOUR

'The Sergeant Major was looking for his teeth'

∽

George Dawson, *born 1921, Kendal.*

Pte G Dawson 3599904
18th Plt, D Coy, 4th BN, The Border Regiment
September 1939.

All my mates were older than me and in the TA. That left me on my own when they were training on a Wednesday and Sunday. So I went and joined, even though I was under age. I got my uniform and had been in the TA about four or five weeks, when the Colour Sergeant said to me, "Have you been passed by the doctor? You can't officially join the Territorial Army until you've been passed." So I went to see the doctor. He examined me and said everything was fine and then, "Oh, there's just one thing. Have you ever had a serious illness?" I told him I'd had Bright's Disease the previous year. "Oh God," he said, "you'll never fit in the army." Back to the Drill Hall I went and handed all my kit in as I shouldn't have been in the TA.

Anyway, about another twelve months went by and every Wednesday and Saturday, I was still on my own. So I thought I'd have another go at joining the TA. I went back down to the Drill Hall and the same Colour Sergeant says, "Don't I know you?" Oh, I answered, "I often see you up street." He knew who I was but just told me I'd have to be passed by the doctor. So I goes down to see the doctor who, of course, didn't remember me. "Oh, everything's fine," he said when he examined me. Then, "Have you had a serious illness?" "I've never ailed a thing in my life." I answered. This time I was in the TA and that was it.

It was the 4th Battalion, Border Regiment at Kendal, I was in. The Battalion Headquarters were at Kendal, along with D Company, which was the Infantry Company, and the drum and fife band, the official military band. As far as I know, it was the first battalion in England to recruit to double its strength. That was in early 1939 when there was these rumours about war.

It was at the time that the Government decided to bring in six months Militia Service. Well, a lot of blokes who were in work didn't want to be called up. But if they joined the TA instead, they could still be at work, you see. So that's why there was a big influx into the TA. It was to miss being called up by the Militia. About the same time, blokes who had been up at court were given the option of going to jail or joining up. So they joined the army and quite a lot gave their wrong names and ages, but I've never asked why.

It was on the cards there was going to be a war. No doubt about it. But I didn't expect it to occur as soon as it did. I remember when we were called up. It was a few days before 3 September 1939. I was working at Craghill's the motor engineers, at Kendal, and had gone across to the newsagent's to buy twenty Gold Flake (cigarettes)for our foreman. When I was at the newsagent's it came on the news (wireless) that all reservists and territorials had to report back to their depots and bases. I went back to

Craghill's and said to my mate, "Jack, we've been called up." The tools went into the toolbox and we said to the boss, "We're off." Down we went to the Drill Hall and were among the first there. Immediately we were put on guard outside the Hall. So that was my calling up.

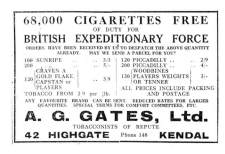
WESTMORLAND SOLDIERS' TOBACCO FUND

cartoon, drawn by Private D Phillips, Kendal, who is "Somewhere in France" with the British Expeditionary Force, underlines local troops' appreciation of cigarette supplies received from the Tobacco Fund.

I was on fire picket one night shortly after our call-up and we had five rounds of ammunition and a pick shaft. Now, the guard had rifles but no ammunition. It was just stupid. When the Orderly Officer came round, I said, "Excuse me, Sir, but what are we supposed to do with these five rounds? Throw them up and hit them with our pick shafts?" I got CB (Confined to Barracks) for that remark.

Our Battalion was so big, they'd had two summer camps for us down at Halton, near Lancaster. I'd been to the first camp, and when we were called up, half the battalion was still at the second camp. But TA lads from Carlisle, Penrith and other places all had to come down to Kendal. There wasn't enough accommodation for everybody so local lads were billeted at home. The rest were billeted in big houses round about and the Parish Hall. One cookhouse was at the Conservative Club and another one at Wilkinson's Organ Works.

After a while the Battalion was split in half, and along with others I was sent up to Carlisle to guard 14 M U (No. 14 Maintenance Unit, Royal Air Force, Carlisle.) That was Rockcliffe, Cargo and places like that. We went up to Carlisle by train and then RAF wagons took us to these different places we had to guard, even though the buildings were empty. We stayed in a sort of police house at the entrance to the Rockcliffe site. The half of the battalion sent up to Carlisle were lads who were under eighteen-and-a-half years old and the ones over forty-five. A lot of the older ones were First World War veterans who were still in the TA. These veterans soon sorted us lads out and taught us to play Pontoon and Crown and Anchor. They would have you play, and as young lads we had nowt else to spend our money on but we never yet won at cards.

At Rockcliffe, we each had a rifle and five rounds of ammunition to guard the perimeter for two hours at a time and then four hours off duty. It was getting near the back end (winter), and half the time we were supposed to be guarding this perimeter, we were down in the heating ducts to keep warm. We did that because we knew what time the officers all came round to check up on us.

We'd only been up at Rockcliffe a couple of months or so, when we were told we'd get a rum ration. Well, this rum ration landed (arrived), two or three big jars to a site. Us young lads filled our tin mugs up with rum and supped it like tea. We were all kalied (drunk) and none of us were fit to be on guard. I think others were brought in to do duty. The next morning, we were all taken down to the HQ, which was at an aerodrome. Captain Baron, a Kendal fella, he read the Riot Act. He said we could all be shot for not being fit for duty.

About this same time, we were having trouble with our food. We got some awful meat. It was all fat and gristle. We'd had to chose one of our lads from the battalion to be cook when we arrived at Rockcliffe. He'd never done any cooking but he did his best. The quartermaster would be paying for good stuff but we were getting all the rubbish. Somebody was getting a backhander or a rake-off out of it. They were dumping anything on us, and we refused to do duties because of that. Again, we were taken off to the aerodrome and the Riot Act was read to us. Within a couple of days, a wagon arrived at Rockcliffe and we were told, "Everybody onto the wagon, who's not on guard." We thought we were going to be shot for refusing to do duty. Anyway, we were taken down to the Co-operative Cafe at Botchergate in Carlisle. We gets in there and had our breakfast with waitress service. And that's what we had for the rest of our time at Carlisle. Breakfast, dinner and tea at the Co-operative Cafe.

I think the final straw up at Carlisle, and probably why we were sent back to Kendal, was we refused to do PT (Physical Training). We flatly refused to do it as we were jiggered. We were on guard duty you see, two hours on and four hours off. So we never got a proper night's sleep, let alone go into Carlisle. Again, the Riot Act was read out of the army book of Rules and Regulations. We had mutinied, and you can be shot for that. Well, we didn't give a damn.

It was the beginning of January 1940 when we came back to Kendal. I remember the first parade we did when we returned. It was a Brigadier's Inspection at the Parish Hall and snow was on the ground. The Sergeant Major was from the First World War and he was a grand fella. But when he shouted out the order to come to attention, his false teeth fell out into the snow. That was the parade finished because the Sergeant Major was looking for his teeth.

We were billeted in a big house at Hawesmead Avenue, outside of town, which later burnt down. I was only up at Hawesmead Avenue for three days. I'd come into town and been in the Angel pub having a pint or two with some mates. When we came out of the pub, the pavement was rutted with frozen snow and I slipped. The next thing I knew, I woke up in the County Hospital with a broken ankle. I had to go to the MO (Medical Officer) with my foot in plaster. He signed me off and I was sent home on sick leave.

I had a good start to the war, I had. I was on crutches but used to meet my mates every night when they finished parade. Above Monatgue Burton's, the tailors, was a wet canteen, which meant it sold beer. We used to go up there and one wet night, coming down the steps, my crutch slipped. Well, the plaster broke and so did my ankle again. It was up to the hospital for another plaster. Another month went by and I went to the Roxy Cinema one night with my mates. Coming down the cinema steps, my crutch went again. Down I went, the same broken ankle and back up to the hospital.

George, now fit after his 'accidents'

"Are you coming to the Town Hall Dance? You can sit up on the balcony," said my mates. "Well, I thought, "I can't get into any trouble there." So I goes and sits on the balcony and watched the dancing. Every time one of the lads goes out for a drink, they brought me a bottle back. By the time the dance finished and I got up to go home, I was stewed. I fell down the steps and broke my ankle for the fourth time. I was never in sick quarters. I was at home having the time of my life. But this time, I had to go to the Commercial Hotel (later the Kendal Hotel), where a Court of Enquiry was set up to see if I'd been guilty of self-inflicted injuries. Anyway, they took my word for it and that was that. Off I went to join the battalion, which had moved to Malton in Yorkshire.

With being stationed in England, we used to come home every twelve months when we got leave. I couldn't tell you if Kendal had changed. All we thought about was going up into the Woolpack Hotel. We always made for the back bar of the Woolpack and gathered there. One night I went in and who should walk in but Bernard Coles, who'd transferred out of the 'Borders' to the Palestine Police. We were having a natter and the next bloke who walks in was Terry O'Conner, a fighter pilot. Finally another bloke joined us who was high up in the navy. When they knew I was going back from leave the next day, it was "You're not going back. We'll sign your pass and say you can't travel because of snow." Well, the nearest snow was at Sedbergh but they all signed my pass so that we could have another three nights out together. When I got back to camp, I was put into the guardroom until my pass was read. It said, "Unable to travel because of snow", signed by a member of the Palestine Police, a fighter pilot and somebody from the navy. I got off with that. Happy days.

When the war finished and I was demobbed, I walked into the canteen on Preston Railway Station. Through the other door came three Kendal lads. They'd just got back from a prisoner-of-war camp and I was the first bloke they'd seen from Kendal. I'll never forget that. It was a wonderful feeling. You see, the street where I live now, I don't think there was a house that didn't have a lad either killed or taken prisoner. *The Westmorland Gazette* used to be full of it. The Town of Missing Men, they called Kendal. That was the Border Regiment lads who went with the Expeditionary Force to France. Most had either been killed or taken prisoner, and people got very bitter about it. It made a mess of this town.

I don't know about any black market during the war, but there was one after the war. One evening I went over to Dent with a commercial traveller who was wanting to buy some eggs. We finished up with about twenty-four dozen eggs and two hams. Just as we were coming back into Sedbergh I said, "Oh God, we've fallen right into it." There on the bend in the road was a police check. Petrol was still rationed at this time and I suppose the police thought if anybody was up that way at night they were up to no good. The policeman who came over to our car knew me and greeted me by my nickname saying, "Hello Jumbo, what are you doing up this way?" "Well," I answered, "we've been up here for a few eggs and a couple of hams. We've got twenty-four dozen eggs in the back and two hams." The policeman laughed as he thought I was joking. He waved us on saying, "Bugger off." If we'd been caught, we would have been sent down (to prison) for I don't know how long. I didn't go for any more eggs.

Long after the war, a few blokes and me got to calling at the New Inn in Kendal for a drink on a Saturday night. We decided to form a little club of our own and called it the Border Fellowship. What we liked about it was, anybody could join who'd taken part in the war. It didn't matter what regiment you'd been with or if you'd been in the Home Guard, Merchant Navy or whatever, you could be a member. Before we knew where we were at, everybody was wanting to join. Then one night, two fellas came in from Bolton who were working up this way. They'd been in the Border Regiment and really enjoyed our tatie-pot suppers at the Fellowship. So they had a 'do' at Bolton and invited us down there. We had a right good night and decided to re-open our local branch of the Border Regiment Association. Anybody from the Fellowship was an honorary member.

By 1962, our families had grown up and we did away with hot-pot suppers and had dinner dances so we could take our wives with us. Our Border Regiment Association got so big there would be six or seven coach-loads of us going to a supper dance, as well as people travelling in their own cars. You see, the thing was about being in any of the forces or war-time organisations, you made friends with people you're with constantly. You found they were good friends and more like brothers because you were together all the time. With all these lads, we were a big happy family.

After the war George did a variety of work and was secretary of the Kendal branch of the Old Comrades Association and branch secretary of the National Union of Public Employees. Now widowed and retired, George has done voluntary work and is a self-taught local historian.

C.1960s George with some of his military memorabilia
(note the hairstyle!!)

FIVE

'Hurricanes, Spitfires and Blenheims came to our farm'

∽

William Herbert Bainbridge, *born 1922 at Woodside Farm, Penrith.*

Yes, we had an idea war was coming. Well, when the Munich scare was on and Chamberlain waved his little bit of paper, 'Peace in our time', we had an idea there wasn't going to be peace.

I was living with my parents at Woodside Farm, which is just three-and-a-half miles out of Penrith, towards Appleby. In them days we had three regular farm workers who were married men, and they stayed with us all through the war. We also had a farm at Eamont Bridge which my grandfather and uncle looked after. They had cattle, sheep and pigs, whereas Woodside was arable.

At that time West Cumberland Farmers collected our eggs for sale, and I joined their organisation as a member just when the war started. If you bought feed or different stuff from them, you got paid back so much in the pound. You were told by the Ministry (of Agriculture) what to grow on the farm. Potatoes mostly. Well, we already grew potatoes, about thirty acres in them days.

We had a couple of wagons and were allowed to use them without licences. It was one pound a year insurance, but we were exempt from licences. Even after the war, you got exempt for six miles a week if you had a wagon that was being used between farms. Well, we had the two farms and we were still exempt.

There was a bit of a black market. I know one fella who used to do a bit. Well, in those days, you'd get jail for the black market. Anyway, the police went to his house so he sent his wife to the door to keep them talking. And there he was, running across to the hen-house, carrying half a pig at a time to hide. Even some of the police were as bad. One was a devil and would do owt to get eggs.

So many of our fields were taken off us to build an aerodrome (Whinfell) on the farm. Somebody from a ministry came and just said they were going to do it. It would take about nine months to build the runway and everything. They didn't put concrete down, it was just ordinary grass and rolled hard. Steamrollers were used to go over it, and farmers got paid so much an hour to roll the ground.

There was only one hangar on the aerodrome. It's still there and it's

Herbert C.1942
at Penrith

used as a grain-drying place. Now the planes, they were sent from Silloth to get repaired. I used to be hoying turnips in one field when all these planes were in the next one. The mechanics were lying in the sun, sunbathing on the planes and I'd be working away and sweat pouring off me.

Hurricanes, Spitfires and Blenheims came to our farm. They came from an operations station to get done up after they'd been in action. Some had been shot up, with their rear gunners killed in the back. And some were in a terrible mess. It was only single or two-engined planes that landed. Though there was one four-engined bomber came, and it shouldn't have done, because two engines were supposed to be the maximum. The officer who was staying with us, it was his mate who was piloting this big four-engined Lancaster. He'd dropped in to pick this officer up and take him down to the Midlands, somewhere.

There was a wood near the runway where they made places to park the planes. Then camouflage net was pulled down over the top of them so it looked well hidden. But we were listening to the wireless one night at the farm and Lord Haw-Haw (William Joyce) came on. He was talking away and then said, " ... and the people of Little Whinfell needn't think they're safe. We know they've got an aerodrome there."

There wasn't many RAF personnel at the aerodrome, just officers and the staff were local civilians. A canteen was specially made for the mechanics and staff. The offices used to be in a tin hut. We had a farm man lived in it, once over. Tin House we called it. A three-bedroomed house, made of wood and lined with tin. After the war part of it was turned into a German prisoner-of-war camp.

At first a Manchester regiment came up to guard the aerodrome. While they were there, a Warrant Officer came and stayed at the farm. He used to be up in the morning at six o'clock and run down to the river, which is about a mile away, and jump in. Every morning, winter or summer, he'd do that.

I can remember this warrant officer going round to check on the guards, which were the Manchester lads. Anyway, one of the guards had stopped him and threatened to shoot him. He never went round again when they were on guard. There was some hard boys in that Manchester regiment. When the regiment left, an RAF regiment with dogs, were sent to act as guards. So at our road end, you couldn't get down to the farm unless you had a pass.

I wasn't eighteen when they came round, wanting local blokes to join the Local Defence Volunteers (LDV). It wasn't the Home Guard then, that came later. In the LDV, you were given an armband and sent out with a shot-gun, a twelve-bore shot-gun, because there wasn't any rifles. Instead of ordinary cartridges with pellets, we were given a few bore cartridges with one ball inside. Now, you had to fire them out of the right-hand barrel. If you fired them out of the left, it would split your barrel up and blow your hand off.

At first in the LDV you were sent out two at a time on patrol. We were on push-bikes with our twelve-bore over our shoulders. You were told to watch for any paratroopers coming down. Well, we had nothing if they had come down. It was awful, a waste of time really. You had this armband clapped on your arm with 'LDV' written on. That was supposed to be if the Germans came and you were taken prisoner, they wouldn't shoot you out of hand. But it wouldn't have done any good, we were still in civilian clothes.

Six months after we'd been in the LDV, we got First World War American rifles. Mine was an Eddison that had a big, long bayonet with a groove in it. For these guns, you had five rounds of ammunition. Like, if the Germans had come, you had five shots to get them. Then, nearly a year after, we got handgrenades and Browning automatics.

26		NOT TO BE PUBLISHED
G.S. Publications		The information given in this document is not to be communicated, either directly or indirectly, to the Press or to any person not holding an official position in His Majesty's Service.
338		

HOME GUARD

INSTRUCTION No. 15—1940

COMMON GERMAN MILITARY EXPRESSIONS

English	German	Pronunciation
Halt! Who goes there?	Halt! Wer da?	HARLT. VAIR DAR?
Hands up!	Hände hoch!	HENDER HOCH.
Come closer!	Kommt hierher!	KOMMT HEAR-HAIR.
Surrender.	Ergebt euch	AIRGAYBT OICK.
Do not shoot.	Nicht schiessen	NICKT SHEESSEN.
Throw down your arms.	Waffen hinlegen.	VAFFEN · HIN-LAYGEN.
Stand still.	Stehen bleiben.	SHTAYEN BLYBEN.
Go in front of me.	Vorausgehen.	FOR-OWSE-GAYEN.
Forward!	Vorwärts!	FOR-VAIRTS.
At once!	Sofort!	· SOFORT.
Double!	Marsch! Marsch!	MARSH MARSH.
Faster!	Schneller!	SHNELLAIR.
Slower!	Langsam!	LANGSUM.
Left!	Links!	LINKS.
Right!	Rechts!	WRECHTS.
Stop!	Halt!	HARLT.
Come back!	Kommt zurück!	KOMMT TSOORICK.

NOTE.—The pronunciation given in Column 3 is the nearest English equivalent to the German sounds. The exact pronunciation can only be learned from a German speaker.

Prepared under the direction of
The Chief of the Imperial General Staff.

THE WAR OFFICE,
20th September, 1940.

There was regular drill and target practice in the fields. On winter nights we were in the barn, doing drill and bayonet practise. I got to be a crack shot getting ten out of ten bulls every time. So I was given extra petrol to go round different Home Guard companies and take them on in competitions.

Half-a-crown a month we were paid in the Home Guard. Fighting allowance it was supposed to be. That's why we had these pay books, you see, to prove we were regulars if we were captured. Mind you, if the Germans had come, we would have been put down straight away.

Oh yes, we did marching. One Friday night we had a dance on, at Brougham Institute. From there we had to set off and march on an exercise. We marched till we got to Lowther Park and got fed. Then on over the moors to Mardale Dam. We were supposed to be guarding the dam, but us young ones thought we'd go down to Bampton for a drink. So we run down to the pub, and when we came back and got laid down, the next thing was a boot in your ribs. "Time you were on guard." We'd already been on guard earlier, but it was, "Well, you can do it again and the old men can lie where they are." From there we marched back to Askham, had range practice, marched back to Brougham, and started work at six o'clock in the morning.

Another time the Home Guard were in Penrith having a dinner at the old Penrith Co-op cafe. Now, there wasn't much drink in those days, but all through the meal we kept getting these bottles. We kept shoving them under the table, thinking they'd run out of beer. But they kept coming and coming. Well, when we all set off to go home from Penrith, of course, a lot of us were drunk. A policeman helped us out of town and on the way home. What a state to be walking home or going by push bike.

Land Army girls at Temple Sowerby
Herbert's future wife is on the front row, 3rd from the right

Just after Dunkirk, my cousin Eddie joined up and I thought, "I'll go in the Air Force as well." I was accepted and went to Squires Gate, the training place just outside Blackpool. Oh, my mam and dad went crackers. Then my grandfather applied for me to go back home. An officer called me in to his office and said, "Now, you've to go back, as you're more important on the farm. We've got any amount of men here but no arms but we'll call you up when we need you." I hadn't even got into the uniform, just denim overalls. So I went back home. But at that age, you didn't like it.

There was a lot of troops in Penrith and a tank corps up at Lowther. It was a very hush-hush job at Lowther, experimenting with them big lights. You know, the lights that you put on the front of tanks that were supposed to blind the enemy. At night all we could see were big lights, very powerful lights. We didn't know what it was about in them days, it was so secret.

There was also a lot of troop convoys on the main road. The biggest movement was when they were going to Norway. Day after day the troops were going over the military road on their way to Newcastle and then Norway. It was daft Chamberlain (Prime Minister) that sent the troops there. Not equipped properly enough, and we were chased out again.

In 1940 an aunt and uncle wrote to us from Guernsey. This uncle used to be a lighthouse keeper on Guernsey, and they wrote asking if we could take a family in who were being evacuated before the Germans invaded the island. That's how we got our evacuees. It was a Mr and Mrs Le Mesurier and their daughter who left Guernsey just a week before the Germans landed. Mr Le Mesurier was the head post-master in Guernsey and that was his nephew, John Le Mesurier who was in *Dad's Army* on television. They settled at Brougham, no bother, and their daughter got a job at a local fruit merchant's while she was here. After the war finished, they returned home.

It was also in 1940 that we had our first prisoners-of-war working on the farm. They were Italians and they didn't like work. They were brought out to farms from Merrythought Camp on the road to Carlisle. An armed guard came with them, but only once and that was it. They never bothered with the guard after that as I should say the Italians were pleased to be prisoners. They would do anything for cigarettes. Some of them already did speak English, but the others learnt and you got to communicate no bother. But for picking potatoes, they would use just one hand with a glove on. There was only one, a Senegalese, a black man, who was any good. Before I got to dig potatoes up with the machine, he had the taties dug up with a fork, he was that frightened. He was a massive, big man and I was more frightened of him. But the Italians themselves, oh, a dead loss.

By '45 there were Germans working for us. Now, they were the best workers. We had one field of potatoes, about eighteen acres, and ten Germans picked them potatoes in a week. The Italians a few years before, we had twenty of them in the same field and it took them a fortnight. One German fella of about fifty, he worked on our farm for a bit. It was loose hay we were forking up. I was above him on the cart and he was forking up to me and he wouldn't stop. We told him to steady on but he wouldn't, and sweat was streaming from him. Later, we found out that he'd been frightened as he'd been told that the British would kill the Germans when they were captured. That's what the Nazis did, like. Said we were bad, same as we said they were bad.

My first wife had been a seamstress from Bolton in Lancashire. She joined the Land Army and was sent up to Temple Sowerby. Her job was to drive the other Land Army lasses round to the farms in a Ford van and that's how I met her. If we wanted to go to the pictures, we'd take some of the other lasses and I'd drive them, as being a civilian, I couldn't have got petrol for myself.

We were married in 1945 and the German officers (P.O.W.s) invited us to a concert they'd put on. So me and my wife and other locals went to this concert which was in a hangar. The German officers would take you in, click their heels and bow when you sat down. They were very, very polite and gave you a good do, like. There were singers and all sorts. Aye, it was all right. Then by 1948 they got repatriated.

There were Polish people here (Penrith) during the war, but not so many of them. When the war finished, more came. Displaced persons (DPs) they

Brougham Hall Camp for Displaced
Persons in Winter C.1947

were, and besides the Poles there were Latvians and other East Europeans. They were put up here at Penrith in huts, army huts, and a lot of them worked on the farms.

When you wanted the DPs to work on the farm, you applied to the War Executive Committee for labour, which cost a shilling an hour. Then, at the end of every month, the War Executive would send you the bill. We applied for extra labour and got Latvians, Ukrainians and Estonians. A lot of them were farmers' sons, so they were good workers.

Area under crops and grass: Cumberland

TABLE 19 — At the June census each year — Acres

Crops, grass and rough	1945	1946	1947	1948	1949
grazings: Total	844,775	845,450	844,418	842,770	841,199
Crops and grass: Total	481,794	482,824 (a)	485,422	484,487	482,221
Arable land	267,732	265,223	257,533	258,729	250,385
Permanent grass	214,062	217,601	226,429	225,758	231,836
Rough grazings	362,981	362,626	358,996	358,283	358,978
Crops and fallow: Total	139,133	132,553	126,147	126,124	121,000
Wheat	5,747	2,906	4,310	4,665	2,464
Barley	4,542	2,399	1,719	1,112	656
Oats	77,810	79,208	75,237	73,737	72,339
Mixed corn	3,818	4,071	4,606	5,302	5,792
Rye for threshing	115	67	44	73	34
Rye for green fodder	22	18	44	22	11
Beans for stockfeeding	251	248	243	260	306
Peas for stockfeeding	49	62	50	78	42
Potatoes, first earlies	1,154	1,438	1,534	1,832	1,416
Potatoes, main crop and second earlies	13,083	12,973	12,286	13,858	11,076
Turnips and swedes for stockfeeding	22,894	21,493	18,840	18,590	19,480
Mangolds	1,797	1,987	1,492	1,855	1,644
Sugar beet	106	89	32	108	64
Rape	3,550	2,198	2,298	1,449	2,201
Cabbage, kale, savoys, and kohl rabi for fodder	1,702	1,541	1,444	1,532	1,690
Vetches or tares	92	78	78	62	88
Mustard for seed	—	8	—	—	—
Mustard for fodder or ploughing in	12	8	17	10	24
Linseed	28	22	32	146	46
Flax for fibre	}	—	—	—	—
Hops		—	—	—	—
Orchards with crops, fallow or grass below the trees	275	249	233	232	224
Orchards with small fruit below the trees (see also tables 191 to 197)	11	7	22	23	25
Small fruit not under orchard trees (see also tables 191 to 197)	32	40	60	46	59
Vegetables (excluding potatoes) grown in the open (see also tables 163 to 182)	870	779	686	721	587
Crops under glass (see also table 183)	20	18	15	18	25
Flowers grown in the open (see also tables 184 to 186)	29	40	44	56 (b)	50
All other crops	218	238	200	160 (b)	153
Bare fallow	906	368	581	177	504
Clover and rotation grasses: Total	128,599	132,670	131,386	132,605	129,385
For mowing	63,451	65,144	68,382	66,016	66,810
For grazing	65,148	67,526	63,004	66,589	62,575
Permanent grass: Total	214,062	217,601	226,429	225,758	231,836
For mowing	47,262	47,431	51,222	50,911	50,069
For grazing	166,800	170,597	175,207	174,847	181,767
Rough grazings: Total	362,981	362,626	358,996	358,283	358,978
Sole rights	261,394	260,731	257,101	256,388	256,396
Common	101,587	101,895	101,895	101,895	102,582

(a) Includes 1,460 acres returned as "Land temporarily out of use through flooding."
(b) Includes 40 acres returned under the heading "Fruit and vegetables grown for consumption by persons living on the holding."
NOTE: Total area of Cumberland (excluding water) 961,554 acres.

Livestock on agricultural holdings: Cumberland

TABLE 20 — At the June census each year — Number

Cattle and calves: Total	1945	1946	1947	1948	1949
Cattle and calves: Total	216,429	213,617	209,000	217,354	224,496
Cows and heifers in milk	56,685	56,498	55,782	57,502	59,897
Cows in calf but not in milk	15,406	15,273	16,187	15,789	15,270
Heifers in calf with first calf	19,911	21,976	20,982	23,869	24,417
Bulls for service	3,288	3,254	3,249	3,491	3,534
Bulls (including bull calves) being reared for service	2,809	2,718	2,690	2,862	2,210
Other cattle:					
Two years and over:					
Male	10,884	10,718	9,438	10,107	9,127
Female	19,018	-18,721	20,114	18,756	18,075
One year and under two:					
Male	10,606	9,208	7,728	6,551	8,832
Female	30,506	30,999	29,431	28,641	30,157
Under one year:					
Male	11,356	9,037	7,702	11,257	12,918
Female	35,960	35,215	35,697	38,529	40,059
Sheep and lambs: Total	546,823	551,649	433,452	489,644	514,159
One year and over:					
Rams for service	6,236	6,469	5,826	5,773	6,104
Ewes for breeding	207,362	212,169	173,786	188,756	193,707
Two tooth (shearling) ewes to be put to the ram	64,534	64,177	51,339	48,527	52,102
Others	57,524	53,809	52,470	52,773	53,411
Under one year:					
Ram lambs intended for service	2,909	2,234	1,754	2,631	2,074
Others	208,258	212,791	149,277	191,184	206,761
Pigs: Total	12,890	11,570	9,894	15,074	16,597
Sows for breeding: Total	1,411	1,243	1,018	2,003	1,939
Sows in pig	555	524	471	840	956
Gilts in pig	356	251	210	641	421
Other sows for breeding	500	468	337	522	562
Barren sows for fattening	157	146	109	131	194
Boars for service	103	79	62	85	90
Young boars being reared for service	..	..	13	49	24
All other pigs:					
Five months and over	3,191	3,007	3,267	3,289	4,386
Two to five months	5,498	4,699	3,776	6,386	6,669
Under two months	2,530	2,396	1,649	3,131	3,295
Poultry: Total	825,312	834,833	793,625	952,180	1,086,075
Fowls: Total	752,460	764,424	732,261	879,200	1,012,151
Six months and over	347,281	380,501	400,279	409,319	488,983
Under six months	405,179	383,923	331,982	469,881	523,168
Other poultry: Total	72,852	70,409	61,364	72,980	73,922
Ducks	33,800	32,313	26,375	28,378	28,811
Geese	21,426	20,284	17,509	22,131	24,266
Turkeys	17,626	17,812	17,480	22,130	20,845
Horses: Total	16,434	16,379	15,563	14,520	12,376
Horses used for agricultural purposes (including mares kept for breeding)	10,584	10,400	9,976	10,034	8,937
Unbroken horses one year and over	2,899	2,971	2,939	2,382	1,640
Light horses under one year	171	98	121	112	125
Heavy horses under one year	1,221	1,165	905	805	647
Stallions for service	123	117	102	101	74
Other horses	1,531	1,628	1,520	1,086	953

One Christmas we had some DPs on the farm who were cleaning the inside of turkeys out. I went out to put these insides on the midden and there, on top of the midden, was a DP. He was cutting fat from the guts that had already been thrown there, to take back to the camp to eat. Oh, they were getting plenty to eat at their camp at Brougham but hadn't had enough at other camps before they came here. So they would do anything for extra food. If there was anything they thought was going to waste, they would take it, you see.

I hadn't been certain we would win the war. We were a year on our own, you know, when France gave up. But when the Germans invaded Russia I knew we'd win. Yes, I knew then we would definitely win.

I mentioned that I'd put five pounds in West Cumberland Farmers during the war to be a member. I never put a halfpenny more in. I just sold the shares about three weeks ago. From that five pounds I got over one thousand, two hundred pounds. That five pounds grew, and when it came to maturity, there was about eight hundred pounds. So that was switched over to shares. Then I thought I might as well sell them instead of letting them lie there. And that's what I got. One thousand, two hundred pounds.

And the bore cartridges from the LDVs, I just left them in my pocket. After the war, I was out shooting rabbits and slipped a cartridge into the gun. When I fired, the barrel split open. It didn't come right to the top of the barrel, or it would have had my hand off. But I've still got the mark where it cut my fingers. I was very, very lucky.

A farmer until retirement, Herbert was a widower
with a family until remarriage.

SIX

'Thank goodness for the British Tommy'

∽

John Ainsworth Brown and his wife Margaret were both born at Barrow-in-Furness.

John C.1942

MARGARET: I definitely remember war being declared in 1939. Mother, Father and myself were on holiday at St Anne's on Sea. My parents decided to cut the holiday short and come home when it was obvious that war was going to be declared.

JOHN: By coincidence, my mother and father and I were also on holiday, but in the south-west of the country at that time. I'd just left the Barrow-in-Furness Grammar School for boys after I'd taken the school certificate. My father got permission for me to leave school early and work in his office. He was Managing Director of the firm, O.M. Huartson Ltd. This firm supplied coal, coke and lime to places like Vickers', the steelworks, hospitals and electricity works.

MARGARET: The first year of the war was my last year at the Grammar School. School-leaving age was fourteen, but if you went to the Grammar School you had to stay on until you were sixteen. The beginning of the war didn't appear to make much difference at school. We carried our gas masks but of course, during the first year of the war, we weren't affected at Barrow.

My father was a trained engine mechanic at Carlisle. He came to Barrow during the First World War to get experience of submarine engines. His intention was to go to sea in the submarines but of course, he was in a reserved occupation and couldn't go. So father stayed put in Barrow, working in the shipyard, designing engines. He was still designing engines during the Second World War. However, when ships or submarines first went to sea, Father travelled with them as far as Glasgow. That could be quite hair-raising but it was to ensure the engines were working to his design.

AIR RAID PRECAUTIONS
Fitting of Gas Masks

As already announced these will be fitted this week at the Polling Stations for the Ward in which you reside.

The following Polling Stations will be used and the Ward divided between them as usual.

WARDS	POLLING STATIONS.
WALNEY	Vickerstown School
	Ocean Road School
BARROW ISLAND	Barrow Island School
	St. Patrick's School
HINDPOOL	St. James' School
	Blake Street School
HAWCOAT	Hawcoat School
	Oxford Street School
	Victoria School
NEWBARNS	Mr. Mansfield's Shop Premises, Newbarns Village
	Abbey Road Wesleyan School
	Cambridge Street School
SALTHOUSE	St. George's School
	Sacred Heart School
	Rampside Parish Room
	Roose Day School
	United Methodist Sunday School
RAMSDEN	Holker Street School
	Thwaite Street School
CENTRAL	Presbyterian Hall, School Street
	Rawlinson Street School

INSTRUCTIONS.

1. Hours of Attendance :—THURSDAY - - 2 p.m. to 8 p.m. FRIDAY - - - 10 a.m. to 8 p.m. SATURDAY - - 10 a.m. to 1 p.m.

2. So far as possible families should come together including children over the age of 15. This will save time for everyone. Measuring takes only a moment.

3. It is essential that everyone over 15 should attend to be measured.

4. Invalids and children under 15 will be separately dealt with.

This scheme for rapid measurement is also a basis for distribution in the event of hostilities, and it can only succeed through individual effort.

YOUR PROTECTION IS IN YOUR HANDS.
YOUR CO-OPERATION IS ESSENTIAL.

Town Hall, Barrow-in-Furness.

W. LAWRENCE ALLEN,
Director of Air Raid Precautions.

Printed by the Exors. of J. Milner, Cornwallis Street, Barrow.

Of course, it was the busiest time for my father with his work and he was an air-raid warden too. I think he did, on average, a couple of nights duty a week. But whenever there was a siren, he had to turn out. He covered the New Barnes area and his post was up at St Paul's School.

JOHN: The outbreak of the war affected my father's business. Once Vickers' started making military ships, their work and the supply of the necessary raw materials became of national importance. All the coal was delivered by rail. None by road. Vickers' used to use something like two thousand tons of fuel a month and all of it came by rail. I suppose in an emergency it could have been lorried in from the pits in Yorkshire and Derbyshire, which were the main sources for coal. But not much coal came from West Cumberland. Theirs was industrial coal, which wasn't suitable for Vickers' furnaces. In most cases, it was the Yorkshire coal that was most suitable.

Besides coal, we dealt with coke, anthracite and some lime. I don't know about the lime, but mostly coal, coke and quite a lot of anthracite went to the hospitals and to the steelworks. Again, this was used for heating furnaces of some sort. I rather think all the heating in the North Lonsdale Hospital came from anthracite. It was all solid fuel.

Really, my father wanted me to succeed him in the firm, as I was the last of three brothers, the other two having escaped. My eldest brother, Alan, who was seven years older than me, was in Glasgow at this time, studying to be a dentist. Because he was in the middle of his course and not in very good health, he would have been turned down for the services, anyway. Two years old then me was Kenneth, who had also entered my father's business. He managed to escape down to Birmingham, where he went as an apprentice. As soon as he was old enough, he joined the Fleet Air Arm.

The way things were going, it was obvious there was going to be stricter control with fuel. O.M. Huartson and similar companies found, as the war progressed, that they were losing their independence and business and were eventually nationalised. As time went on, my father recognised this would happen and didn't want me to stay with the firm.

I could easily have gained exemption from the services, but I volunteered for the RAF to escape the office work, which I hated. At first, being too young for the forces, I joined the Air Training Corps. This was held in the County Club, opposite the laundry. Oh, we were all crazy about aeroplanes. Everybody wanted to be a Spitfire pilot. All the young fellows wanted a life of adventure, which is what it was to a seventeen-year-old. The appeal of the fighter pilot was all-consuming.

Us youngsters walked about wearing these Air Training Corps flashes on our hats. We drilled and we had lectures about different kinds of aircraft. How they functioned. What their purpose was in the RAF We had all sorts of military training in a very gentle way, suitable for seventeen-year-olds while we were waiting to join up.

Most of our instructors were RAF officers. There was an RAF establishment on Walney, and officers from there came over and talked to us boys. We didn't go up in these planes in the earlier stages of the war and it wasn't their job to teach us how to fly. The RAF would eventually do that.

Margaret C. 1942

MARGARET: When I left school, I started work the next day. I left school before the end of term because I was offered a job in the Education Department of the Town Hall. Of course, with it being the Education Department, I was allowed to leave school.

Officially I was a trainee clerk at the Education Department but was sort of an office girl or general dogsbody. It wasn't really what I wanted to do. During my last six months at school I'd my name down at the Employment Exchange to become a telephone operator. As I was offered the Education job, I was advised to take it by the Headmistress. My first wage was ten shillings a week. I gave all of it to my mother and she gave me back my pocket money.

JOHN: Like Margaret, I was very much the junior at work. Let me assure you that her starting wage of ten shillings a week was far more than I got. With being the son of the Managing Director it had to be shown that I was not being favoured. I got five shillings a week, which, of course, is twenty-five pence now-a-days.

MARGARET: I was only at the Education Department for three months when I was transferred to the Telephone Exchange and I really did like it. The Exchange was at St Michaelson's Post Office, which had been the General Post Office. Then, just before the war, a new General Post Office was built by the railway station, but they didn't move the telephone exchange.

To start with I had six weeks of intensive training. An emergency exchange had been built down below in the cellars and we were trained in that. So we had a working exchange to train on, and then went upstairs into the main exchange. There, every position had two plugs for your headsets and a trained operator always listened in with you. That was in case you got into trouble or were stuck over anything and she could take over.

About sixteen girls worked on the exchange and we covered from eight o'clock in the morning till eight o'clock in the evening, when men took over. There was a whole series of duties you could be on, including split duties. Of course, once anyone caught a cold, it just went round everybody. Sitting so close to each other, you couldn't avoid contact.

There was no new telephones fitted during the war to private subscribers. New phones had to be for commercial use or to do with the war. And there was very little dialling. But there was what was called an Unit Automatic Exchange. Millom was one and Broughton-in-Furness was another. This meant people could dial a Millom or Broughton number, but that's all they could dial. To call anywhere else, they had to come through to the Barrow Exchange.

From Barrow, our two main outlets for calls were Manchester and Liverpool. That was until the Liverpool Exchange was flattened in the bombing and calls went via Manchester. Even calls to London. If we wanted a Manchester Deansgate number, we would go through to the Manchester operator and ask for the Deansgate number, and she would connect us.

The building we worked in was all right until it was bombed. It was one of those places where the outside wall was mostly big windows. But with bombing the windows were blown out. They never replaced the windows. Just bricked them up and put ventilation bricks very so often.

I suppose the bombing did come unexpectedly. The very first bomb was a one-off. Docker's, the fruiterers, had this orchard, and the green houses in the orchard were hit. That was put down to the moon shining on the greenhouses, which attracted a German plane.

JOHN: The bombing probably started first of all with targets in the south. Plymouth, Portsmouth and the London area. Then Barrow was a logical step after Liverpool. The planes they were using were Dornier 17s and Heinkel 111s, which had drop tanks. These tanks which were fitted under the wings, gave them extra fuel and extra range.

After the bombing at Hawcoat Lane, Barrow-in-Furness

MARGARET: An unexploded bomb fell near to the high level bridge, the main bridge from Barrow to Walney. I happened to be on duty in the exchange, which was very near to the bridge, when the bomb went off. The whole of the switchboard moved towards me and then back again. But we kept going.

It was in 1942 we were bombed out of our house. It wasn't demolished but it was uninhabitable. The five doors (houses) below us were flattened. We had friends on Walney and we parked ourselves on them until a colleague of mine who lived at Broughton-in-Furness found us a place to stay.

JOHN: Our house was not so badly damaged as Margaret's. All the walls were standing but the roof was badly damaged. From the downstairs you could see straight up to the blue skies. We had no friends to whom we could go, and as the walls of our house were still standing we said we would continue sleeping at home. With not having anywhere else to go, we were given priority for the fitting of haystack-type canvas sheets or tarpaulins over the top of the roof. This was to make the house watertight and habitable.

I remember, when all this happened, it was wonderful weather. Blue skies for days and days. There was no rain and not a cloud in the skies. Both

Margaret and I were in our respective homes on the night of the bombing. The next morning, Margaret, who had been sitting against the chimney breast, had a sliver of glass embedded in the wood by her head. Our front door had blown inwards and was alongside of me.

We didn't have Anderson shelters at the time. People used the railway station and schools when they'd been bombed out and had nowhere to go. Others, in good weather, used to go into country to sleep.

MARGARET: We stayed at Broughton-in-Furness for about two years with two very nice people. I had a bedroom to myself and my parents had one. So there was no problem there. With my father and I being at work all day, Mum was left on her own. She just mucked in with everybody. Of course, there

More bomb damage in Barrow-in-Furness

wasn't much to do in the evenings. The earliest I could get back to Broughton was six o'clock at night. I used to get off the train at Foxfield and walk the mile and a bit to Broughton on my own. Of course, in winter it was dark, but you had no fear. There was no fear in those days. You see, there was a comradeliness at that time, and in spite of the bombing, life carried on.

JOHN: The earliest age they would take you in the forces was seventeen and a quarter. I went in the first day I was eligible. I had two or three friends who were going at the same time, and we went to Padgate near Warrington. My brother, Kenneth, was already in the Fleet Air Arm and I saw him when we were both in training.

My longest spell without being able to get home was fifteen months.

John, 'wings' gained C.1944

But towards the end of the war, when we were flying on operations from this country, I was able to get home about every two or three months. A home leave was seven days.

By that time Margaret and I were not yet engaged but heavily courting. I think I can say without fear of contradiction, we were very much in love. We had eyes for each other and very little else during my leave. We used to cycle up to the Lake District. 'Cyclimbing' I used to call it. Cycle to Thirlmere and climb Helvellyn. We loved doing that. It wasn't difficult when I was home on leave to shoot out and find a quite place. Petrol was rationed and you could cycle for miles and not see a car.

Margaret: Barrow was well supplied with cinemas and theatres. You shared your coupons, and clothing didn't cost very much. I never felt as though I was done out of things. As an only one, I never suffered. Obviously we didn't have fancy meals, and we managed. There were shampoos but not the quality or variety that there are now. Actually, I just used soap. Soap and water, then put metal rollers in my hair. Hair wash and bath night was on Friday night.

The indoor and outdoor market in Barrow continued, and it was surprising what there was on them. Though clothing was in short supply, you could usually get what you wanted. Even after the war when clothing was still rationed, someone on Barrow market offered me a length of material to make my wedding dress without coupons.

It was just towards D-Day that the Government said they would pay for repairs to bomb damage. That was when the Council started repairing bomb damage, and as soon as we could, we moved back home. I was working on VE Day, but I can remember VJ Day more clearly. We knew VE Day was coming, and we were given special duties so that we only worked half the day. But VJ Day just sort of happened, so we hadn't been given our duties. Some people turned up for work and some didn't.

JOHN: It was towards the end of the war that the Americans came to Barrow. But I'd like to speak in their defence. I did my flying training in Canada and spent leave in New York. The Americans in their homes are delightful. I don't believe when they are abroad they are any worse than we are.

MARGARET: This will tell you about the Americans. I was waiting on Barrow Station one day for a train to Broughton. A train-load of Americans came in, got off the station and just wandered all over the place and onto the railway lines. They didn't bother where they went, and no two were dressed alike. The chappie who was standing next to me on the platform said, "Thank goodness for the British Tommy." Because British soldiers were always smartly dressed and always came to attention. They wouldn't have wandered all over the place like those Americans did.

JOHN: My brother Kenneth was killed on 1 June 1944, just four days before D-Day. He was on an aircraft carrier which was flying Seafires, the naval version of the Spitfires. Kenneth was flying the planes all us young men wanted to fly. But he was shot down into the sea off Norway escorting a convoy to Russia.

It must have been a horrifying time for my mother. My father wasn't in the Home Guard as he wasn't fit enough. He was badly affected with his lungs, which was a big problem. My eldest brother's health wasn't very good, and Alan eventually died of tuberculosis. Kenneth was killed flying, and I was still flying. It must have been very difficult for her.

I was in the RAF for four and a half years. I'd always been interested in farming and would have liked to have done that instead of working for my father. When I was demobbed, I used the excuse that my education had been interrupted by the war. Like many servicemen did, I got a grant and went to Reading University to study agriculture.

At university, only a very small proportion of students were direct from school. The great majority were ex-service people. We were mostly in our early twenties, and fairly resourceful people who'd had a lot of responsibility during the war. So we felt rather superior to the school leavers. But they were better at studying than we were.

As ex-servicemen we all had the same problem of knuckling down and struggling to study. It was pretty awful, but we were all in the same boat and there was the same sense of comradeship as through the war. Most of us got through the work and after the first year, it wasn't so bad. But I wouldn't have liked to have stayed on at university longer than three years. Besides, I wanted to get married, start a family and get out into the business world.

When I got my degree, I went into farming down south. Eventually, I joined a feedstuff company and became a director. We've lived almost half our lives in the south of England and half in the north. So we feel than we can pontificate about this. It is friendlier up here. That's why we came back.

After the war, John studied at Reading University,
became an agricultural advisor and then a company director.
John & Margaret are now retired with grandchildren.

SEVEN

'There was a friendship during those years'

∞

Eva Kennedy, born Tyne Dock, Tyneside. Worked at No. 14 Maintenance Unit, Royal Air Force, Carlisle during the war years.

To Tom with all my love, Eva
1941

Tom and I married in 1937 and lived in a little flat at Rosehill, Wallsend. By 1939 it was a very traumatic time. Unfortunately we lived near a battery of guns and the German bombers were trying to get this battery. Nearby houses were hit by bombs and some of my friends were killed.

It was a strange experience being in our Anderson shelter in the garden. You could hardly tell the difference between the guns and the bombs because we were so near this gun site. Gun's were blasting away and bombs were coming down. We knew there'd been a hit fairly near because the noise of all the kettles and pans.

I've never heard anybody describe this, but all the debris that was flung up in the air came down with such a force. We could hear the kettles and pans rattling along the street. It was very, very strange when we came out of the shelter. The next street had the front blown out of it. It was like seeing a doll's house when you open the door and all the various rooms are exposed.

When Tom and I came up from the shelter, we had to shovel our way into the flat because of the soot and bricks that had come down the chimney. But the biggest shock was, I'd just done three weeks' washing and all the soot had fallen over my fresh ironing. Can you imagine what that was like? Strangely enough, our budgie was still there. He'd been blown out of his cage. The same blast had blown the cage door open and the budgie out at the same time. Then the cage door had closed behind him. It was incredible, and despite all this, there he was, chirping his head off, absolutely happy.

Shortly after this, Tom was called up and he didn't want me to live by myself. Especially since the windows of the flat were permanently boarded up. So I got in touch with Tom's brother who lived at Carlisle and his landlady said she would take me in. I went through to Carlisle on the train and took my budgie in his cage. It was just like that song, ".. I followed on with my old cock linnet .." only it was a budgie instead.

I couldn't take furniture with me, as there wasn't enough room for any at Carlisle. One friend who needed her front room furnishing borrowed some of mine. Another friend came with a handcart and took all the lino and woollen rugs. We didn't have carpets, only rugs that we made ourselves. So I had only to bring my bedding with me to Carlisle.

The house where I stayed was at Hetherington Road, in the Currock area. I lived in a little room with a single bed. The lady of the house had three children and they were all squashed into one room. My brother-in-law was a joiner, working on the prisoner-of-war sites, and he slept on a settee downstairs.

I was welcomed at Hetherington Road but my main thought was, "I've got to find work." The next day I went straight down to the Labour Exchange and told them what work experience I had. I was given a card and told to go to 14 M.U. (No, 14 Maintenance Unit, Royal Air Force, Carlisle) for an interview and was taken on.

To get to work from Currock, I had to take a bus into town. From there, 14 M.U. laid on buses onto the site because so many people from all directions were coming into Carlisle. Around the headquarters, there were various sites and I was on No.5 Site. It sounds funny, but I didn't know where the other sites were, as everything was hush, hush during the war.

There were M.U.s all over the country. At 14 M.U. there were people from all over and we mixed in fine. The strange thing was, I made five close friends and they were all Tynesiders. It's an affinity with people, isn't it?

We worked in hangars, and the offices were very cold, with stone floors. The only carpet went straight up the centre of the hanger. I think that was for the benefit of the man who came around with the tea trolley in the mornings with our cups of tea.

I was on the Marine Section doing stock control. That was anything to do with spares for small boats. Not warships but the smaller boats that were important and went between these bigger ships. When stock came in, I had to mark it down on record cards or subtract it if stock was going out. You'll know how wide the scope was, as it could be anything from a washer to an engine. But the system was never perfect. For one thing, people used to take things like the odd screw. Or machines got put into the wrong place. Some of the stock was very expensive, so if you made a mistake you were costing the Government a tremendous amount of money. Every so often we had to adjust the figures because they weren't right. But they were a good guide as to what was on site.

Our canteen was a little way off from No. 5 Site and I remember that you got nothing but soup some days. That was when the convoys were being sunk bringing food into the country. It was terrible. During that period we lived mostly on soup and beans in the canteen. We had every kind of bean you can imagine. Pink beans, brown beans. What their names were, I don't know. Terrible, terrible food. The only good thing about it was, you didn't have to use your coupons for canteen meals and I could give them to my landlady.

Every now and again we had concerts on the site and these were very good. It was local talent, a sort of Workers' Playtime. So anyone who could recite or sing or whatever they could do, got up and performed. We also arranged netball matches and I enjoyed playing those. We'd dash and have lunch, then straight onto a flat bit of ground and have a match. Both sexes played and no quarter was given.

I didn't work shifts but I worked overtime. The normal wage was just over three pounds a week. If I worked till eight o'clock for two nights a week and also a Sunday afternoon, I made four pounds and ten shillings. After I finished work on a Saturday afternoon, I'd come into town and go to a cinema or a show.

Most Saturday afternoons I had to go and try to buy my budgie's seed. I bought it from

a little seed shop and it cost four shillings a pound. Can you imagine that? Seed was so scarce with coming from abroad, you were only allowed a few ounces to last a week. But to supplement this, I gathered grasses to feed the budgie and the lady of the house even boiled some rice for him to live on. Mind you, he lived right through the war.

I also used to go to a dance down Botchergate with the lady of the house. A lot of our people from 14 M.U. went there so we used to meet and it was almost like a club. You see, Carlisle was absolutely packed during the war years. There were soldiers and air force men and, later on, the Americans. No, I wasn't very fond of Americans. I didn't trust them and I didn't like their chewing gum. Chew, chew, chew. But poor souls, they were flyers and mostly on duty at Anthorn airfield.

Mind you, the only time I came into contact with them was when two friends asked me to go to their house and meet their American boyfriends. They were nice fellows and were more practical than our men. When I went to the house, these Americans had taken over the cooking and produced a lovely meal for us. My two friends married these Americans and went back to America with them after the war.

There was a friendship during those years. It was marvellous coming home on the bus at night, as we all sang. We used to sing all the war songs and things like, 'She'll be coming round the mountain'. It was super, really. And there were nice shows, and the cinema, and even the ballet. We used to go to Her

To my beloved husband.
From Eva March 1943

Majesty's Theatre and sit high up in the gods. That cost ninepence.

Carlisle was totally different from Wallsend. You see, over at Wallsend we could hear the bombs falling on Newcastle. Then there were the guns going off and air balloons in the sky to try and stop the enemy planes. One day over at Wallsend, the sky was a beautiful blue and there was this dog fight taking place between two planes. I had to lie flat against a wall while all these shells came raining around me. There was nothing like that at Carlisle.

Yes, there was a black market. At one of the digs where I stayed, the landlady's husband was a soldier on duty in Northern Ireland. When he came home he brought loads of things in a big suitcase. Butter, linen hankies, and things like that, which were easy to get hold of in Ireland. Then I remember a shopkeeper, she was sent to jail for selling stolen goods. The chief customers she was supplying food to, were two of her special friends. But she never divulged their names.

Normally everybody had to queue for whatever they wanted. There were queues everywhere and you joined them irrespective of what was being sold. You joined a queue and then you said to your neighbour, "What's the queue for?"

I was never able to get a flat of my own as there were too many people looking for accommodation. The lady of the house where I was staying died, so I moved to near the racecourse where I had some friends. Then I managed to get a room back at Beaumont Road and was there when my husband was invalided out of the forces. That was the beginning of his health troubles.

Tom had been stationed in Iraq all this time and I hadn't seen him for over four years. He'd write part of a letter every day to me and these letters arrived all in batches. We were living in one room at Beaumont Road and then Tom was in hospital for nearly eight months. He was in Padgate Hospital for the RAF personnel, just outside Blackpool.

I remember going to Padgate to see Tom after he'd had an operation. I was eight months pregnant and it was Bank Holiday and no taxis were running. As the hospital was two miles out of Blackpool, I had to walk there and in roasting hot weather. I stayed with Tom until he came round from his operation and by that time it was night and I couldn't get back to Carlisle. So I walked the two miles back to Blackpool, knocking on anybody's door who I thought looked reasonable, saying "Can you take me in for the night?" Well, one lady took me in and showed me up to the bedroom. There was no carpet, just bare boards, and for a light, she lit a flare. Can you imagine, a market flare in a bedroom? It was dangerous. Then I saw that there were clothes scattered around the room, which belonged to some other girl who was away for the weekend. To cap all this, the woman said, "I'm sorry but I've no food in the house, only bread." I was famished by this time and ate the bread. I had to pay eight shillings for the night.

During the war years, I went back to Simonside about every six weeks to see my dad who was a retired railworker. Dad had a housekeeper as my mother had died. It was a very traumatic time for him, as when I was young, he'd had a nervous breakdown and never really recovered. However, he was an air-raid warden and dealing with incendiary bombs. That really finished Dad off and he was never the same again.

After the war, Tom needed an office job, with his health not being very good. So he went to 14 M.U., as a temporary civil servant at first, then passed his exams and was put on permanent staff. A few years later, we moved to various M.U.s all over the country. Tom was only sixty-one when he died and I eventually returned to Cumbria.

14 M.U., Carlisle C.1950
Tom is second from the left

Eva, now a widow with one daughter, lives in Keswick.

EIGHT

'So Dad walked right into the harbour'

∽

John Skelly, born 1913 at Whitehaven, has lived on the Kells Estate since an early age.

With Whitehaven being out on a limb, I don't think the average man round here thought there was going to be a war. No, there wasn't any inclination or sign, and when it started, it was a shock to everybody.

There was the Declaration of War, and things came slowly in. First of all, men who were already in the Territorial Army were taken from the mines. Nobody else was allowed to leave the mines. If you wanted to leave, or say if you got a good job elsewhere, you couldn't leave. The Essential Works Order came in, you see, and you had to stay where you were.

That same order affected discipline in the mine, because if a man misbehaved himself, he couldn't be sacked. I've known of occasions when men were really bad and they were sent up to Bankfield, which was the local HQ of the coal industry's pits in this area. But they were just sent back to work again and that affected discipline.

At that time there was Haigh Pit and William Pit in town (Whitehaven) and other pits in the surrounding area. So there was plenty of work going on but not enough men always to do it. It could create a certain amount of tension as you always got some men who wanted Monday off as they'd been out drinking over the weekend. In the main, pit men always did their job to keep the war effort going.

Normally there were three shifts in the mine, what was known as First, Back (Afternoon) and Nights. But there came a time when shifts were a bit more complicated, because they were trying to push more production work into the day's twenty-four hours. My job at that time was what was known as a 'pan puller', which was a conveyor shifter. This conveyor could be a hundred yards long, and you had to dismantle it, shift it, and rebuild it in the next line of supports. As the coalface was advancing, you would advance the conveyor. But the point is, we would go on our shift and, instead of being able to start at, say, two o'clock when we got to the coalface, the coal hadn't been stripped off, or something had gone wrong. The consequence was, you maybe didn't get started until five or seven o'clock, and yet you had to finish your job so that everything was ready for the next shift.

At this time, the war affected us in a number of ways. The conveyor I'm talking about was one with a rubber belt. A twenty-four inch rubber belt. But you couldn't maintain that width, and new ones were scare. Sometimes it was torn at parts to fifteen inches wide instead of being the full width. So the face workers were loading coal onto a fifteen-inch belt, and it was falling down onto the bottom belt of the conveyor, causing jamming and belt breakages. Also the joining clasps on the end of each section of belting, joining onto one another, should have been put on with copper rivets. With the war being on and the demand for copper, we had to get four-inch nails from the stores, shorten them with a chisel, and use those as rivets. Timber was often in short supply and we used all kinds that wasn't the best, just to keep the work going.

Before the coal left the pits it went up onto moving tables at which women worked who screened coal (removed stones). But women weren't allowed to work there after nine o'clock at night. Work still had to go on, so men used to go onto this job to keep production moving. After the coal was screened it went onto trucks and down to the harbour for shipment to Ireland, or the railway station and on to our own power stations. Quite a lot

Carpentry work at Kells Miners Welfare Club
during the war years

Kells Miners Welfare Club
Cadet work during the war years

of shipping used to come into the dock for the loading of coal or bringing timber, which was essential for mining. Although by this time, they were slowly moving away from using timber to iron supports, as these didn't have to be renewed to the same degree.

Right below where I live now there were pit banks, which were waste heaps that had been tipped over the cliffs over the years and ran right down to the high water mark on the shore. During the day people used to go and pick waste coal from these heaps. But at night-time the pit banks were alight due to spontaneous combustion. So a pipeline had to be brought from the pit. Water was poured onto the heaps both night and day for months in an effort to put out the fires so that enemy planes didn't see them.

Round here like everywhere else, there was a blackout. Shops, houses, everywhere was blacked out and there was quite a number of humorous occasions of people getting lost. My old dad went out of his house at North Row one night and had only to go sixty yards to the main road. Instead of that, he got lost in a little cul-de-sac, called The Nest, and couldn't get out. He found himself against a fence every time he changed direction. Dad was there about an hour before somebody heard him shouting.

Another time Dad came out of a pub, where the new Beacon is now on the harbour. He thought he could see his friend's torchlight in the distance but it was the light across the harbour. So Dad walked right into the harbour and was up to his chest in mud. A policeman came and asked me to go to the home of an old lady who had taken Dad in, and take him some dry clothes. It was the black-out you see, and he had no idea where he was. He wasn't the only one. An old man called Tom from round here (Kells) was heard shouting down from the bottom of the hill, "Can anybody tell me where Toole's pub is?" The pub was about half a mile away at the top of the hill, but he'd got lost.

Here on Kells people were even digging up their little back yards for the war effort, and the number of allotments increased. They grew lettuce, leeks or a few taties. There was an increase in home-made jam, home-made wine, home-made anything, because of the shortage. People went mushrooming in the fields, or onto the shore looking for crabs. Anything to help out with their rations. One of the things that was produced was a friendliness. People would share what they had – broth that they made in quantities, baking, almost everything.

One chap that I knew, Tommy, who lived near here, had three sons. To supplement their rations Tommy would get his sons to chase a sheep from the field and over the cliffs.

CUMBERLAND AND WESTMOR-LAND CONSTABULARY.

POLICE NOTICE.

DEFENCE REGULATIONS.

OWNERS of RACING PIGEONS and HOMING PIGEONS are reminded that no person is permitted to have control of, or liberate, such pigeons unless he holds a PERMIT for this purpose granted by, or on behalf of, the Chief Officer of Police.

Information in connection with such permits may be obtained at any Police Station.

(Sgd.) P. T. B. BROWNE,
Chief Constable
of Cumberland and Westmorland.

Chief Constable's Office,
Penrith.
9th September, 1939.

Then he would go and tell the farmer about this sheep. Well, the farmer was reluctant to go down the cliff for the sheep. So Tommy and his lads would get it and have mutton for quite a while, and some of the meat would be shared out among neighbours.

Another incident around that time was when my dad and his mate Bill, were out catching linnets and finches. Remember, they were miners and would be catching songbirds to be kept at home, though this was forbidden. They saw some movement in the fields and it was a chap, a nearby neighbour, skinning a sheep in the long grass. The chap offered them a piece of the meat to keep quiet. "You won't," says Bill, "I don't just want a bit of it, you'll get me a sheep." So within a day or two, Bill got a skinned sheep he didn't expect to have. Then Bill had to get it home, carefully concealed.

As you'll know, in those days the miners were great ones for keeping pigeons and, of course, many people with allotments had hens. During the war the felting that covers these sheds and huts wasn't available. What people did round here was, they used newspaper or old wallpaper. They would put a sheet of newspaper or wallpaper across the hut and cover it with tar. Then another sheet of paper and cover that with tar, and so on. As a matter of fact, when this covering was eventually taken off, it had set almost like hardboard, it was that thick.

I should tell you a bit about myself. I was a conscientious objector, and so was my younger brother, George. The church we went to at that time was the Brethren Assembly. At the beginning of the war some of us met at the church to decide, as Christians, if it was right or wrong, good or bad to go to war. It was unanimously decided that, as Christians, it wasn't right to kill others. I knew that because I worked in the pits, I wouldn't be taken into the forces, but I registered as a conscientious objector. To me, it would have been a sin not to register since I had a conscience on the matter.

My younger brother, George, was also exempt from joining the forces on condition he stayed at his own job, which was essential war work. However he later volunteered for non-combatant duties. First, he volunteered for the Pioneers (Pioneer Corps), who so often, as conscientious objectors, got all the dirty jobs to do. Then George volunteered for bomb disposal, which at that time was the most dangerous job in the army. After serving there, he volunteered for the paratroops medical section, again in the non-combat section. My brother was dropped into France on D-Day and was wounded on the second day, getting help for his company which had been surrounded. He was, at that time, the only conscientious objector to be decorated for gallantry.

I'm just pointing out that, it brings trials going to war. For others, it brings trials not going to war. You have a conscience, therefore you have a right to stand up for what you consider is right. I worked with over twelve hundred men, and never during the whole of the war did any man say to me that I was a conscientious objector or a coward. I thought that was good, as an objector and coward was synonymous in the minds of many people at that time. The only reason I can think of is that I was sincere in my other work with the sick, children at Sunday School, mid-week religious meetings and visiting the elderly.

I used to visit a lot of people who were sick or children who were absent from Sunday School. Most of them lived in three rows of houses that had been built for miners many years ago by Lord Lonsdale. These were known as New Houses and there was Front Row, Middle Row and Back Row. These were terraced houses, about eighty in each row, and built along the breast of a hill overlooking the town. If you were walking along Middle Row, you could sit on the roofs of the Front Row houses, and if you were walking along Back Row you could sit on the roofs on the Middle Row.

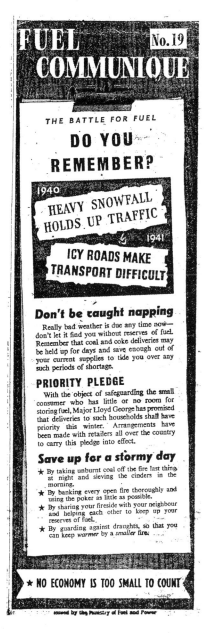

These houses were in steps up the breast of the hillside and were in the parish of Colliery Mission. There was roughly two hundred and fifty houses with sometimes ten or eleven people in one house. The houses weren't built with inside toilets. Instead, for every four or five houses, there was just a little box-like toilet over the other side of the road. Taps were outside as well, with every drop of water to be carried both in and out of the house. You can see what condition people lived in. So there was all these houses on the hill, and across the valley was Lord Lonsdale's castle, in which two people lived with their servants. These houses have been destroyed now, as they weren't fit to live in, and hardly so when they were first built.

During the war there was an increase in church attendance with the sorrow and tragedy that was coming to all different parts of the town. And what was called United Open Air Meetings, where Christian testimony was given, was allowed in Castle Park. Also midweek church meetings were held, and they often had tatie-pot suppers to foster friendship, as well as give sustenance to many.

In my own case, I had a mid-week class of young people from twelve to fifteen years of age and we made baskets, wooden toys and other things that were missing in the shops because of the war. Then once a year there was Sunday School trips and we'd go to somewhere like St Bees or to Seascale. But even with the war on, it was commonplace for people to walk in those days, to St Bees and elsewhere, compared to now. Especially on a Sunday, dozens and dozens of people would be out walking along the cliffs and Whitehaven Pier.

Holidays were a rarity in pit life. You usually had the Bank Holidays, but there wasn't many miners who went on holidays. The opportunities and economics usually prevented them. You see, some were like my dad, who drank, and therefore there wasn't any spare money. For a few, it was the pit, the pub and their bed. And it didn't change with the war. It still went on.

Towards the end of the war we had Bevin Boys come into the pits. They were named after Ernest Bevin who introduced a Bill selecting for work in the mines, those called up for the forces. Selection was made by selecting those who's registration number ended with a certain figure. With the shortage of manpower, we got men from all works of life, both locals and people from away. One chap later went on to be a minister, and another, a teacher. The one who became a minister had a friend with him who could swallow razor-blades and chew glass allies. Allies were glass marbles that were used as stoppers on lemonade bottles.

Because of the Bevin Boys, it was the beginning of over-manning in a sense. One would be sent to fetch a pit prop and it was, "Oh, I'm not going for that." And you couldn't do anything about it, so you had to send another man with him. Since these young men were immature miners, you were sending two men for what was one man's job, simply because one was a Bevin Boy.

One of the extra jobs that the miners volunteered to do, as so many of the men were away fighting, was fire watching at hospitals or other important buildings. I was one of the fire watchers at the local hospital, usually one night a week. You had to go, say seven o'clock at night, depending on the time of year, summer or winter, and stay until the next morning. Then you'd probably be at work that morning or afternoon.

There was very little activity, not like down at Barrow-in-Furness where there was a large shipyard. We didn't have much trouble with enemy aircraft but you had to be alert, that was the point. You could never tell when something might happen. In the latter end of the war, it got that three or four chaps would sleep at night while on fire-watching duty. Another chap would be alert ready to wake the others if anything was likely to happen.

Yes, there was street parties when the war ended. People celebrated because it meant a lot to them. They thought, "War's finished. Everything will be the same as it used to be." But it took years and years to get back to anything like normal. Rations and the limitations on clothes or shoes you could buy went on for a long time. Really, everything went on the same for a long time after the war. In fact, the end product of the war has been a disappointment. It hasn't been a land fit for heroes to live in. These days it takes a hero to live in it.

PHOTOGRAPH: JONATHAN BECKER, AGT LTD, CARLISLE

A recent photograph of John beside the
miners memorial at Whitehaven

John, now a retired miner, married with one daughter,
is a lay-preacher, writer, poet and fund-raiser for charity.

NINE

'Nobody wanted these two children'

∽

*Alice, born in 1908 at Grange-over-Sands
but living in Kendal during the war years.*

I didn't know the war was going to start because I'm not a political animal, so it was quite a shock when it did start. You sort of heard rumblings going on but Mr Chamberlain (Prime Minister) waved his piece of paper about 'Peace in our time' and of course we believed him.

Jack, my husband had previously been out of work for quite a long time, and when the war started he was a caretaker at some public buildings. It was an unskilled job and the powers that be must have looked up Jack's record, saw that he was an engineers' fitter, and he was directed to Barrow shipyard. Of course it wasn't too far away, but he was in digs and only came home about once a month.

Jack worked strange hours because he was directed to work on the submarines and therefore was working in the submarine dock. Well, they weren't allowed to start work before nine o'clock on a winter's morning because they couldn't have any lights on which would be visible from the air. They also had to stop work before three o'clock in the afternoon for the same reason. Sometimes Jack's hours were even less than that. So, as a result, instead of him being able to pay for his board and digs, I often had to send Jack money because his wage wasn't enough. You see, he was just working short time and it meant that light was the deciding factor in his working hours. However we had very, very little in savings, because he'd been out of work for a long time before the war. But we managed. Quite honestly, we managed very well.

We had only one child, Gordon, who was a baby at that time, so I had my name down for an evacuee. Everybody round about got an evacuee except me, and I was quite disappointed. The

following night at about half past ten there was a knock on the door and it was a man with two evacuees in his car. He said that he'd been all round the county and nobody wanted these two children and - this is the remark I still find very offensive - "Just come to the car and have a look at them, but it's all right if you don't want them." I felt there would have been more kindness shown to stray animals.

I went to look at these two children and it was a pitiful sight. They were brother and sister, Joan was about nine years old and Ian was seven. She was crying with tiredness. They'd probably set off about seven that morning from the North East with their sandwiches and had nothing to eat since arriving in our area. I'd only wanted one child but I offered to have both. You couldn't separate them.

It wasn't until later I found out that Joan must have had TB because the special school she'd attended at South Shields was an open one without any windows. I do think somebody should have told me because Gordon, my own son, was only nine months old at the time. I know it's indelicate but one thing that did happen was Ian wet the bed. It caused extra work, but I never did chide him, as it was nervous strain, and eventually he grew out of it.

Oh, both the children settled in well. Their whole class along with their teacher was evacuated to Kendal. I can remember the teacher's name was Miss Golightly, and after the war she retired to Kendal because she liked the area. Out of school hours we had some wonderful times because we'd go out at weekends for picnics, then up High Line for train-spotting or for a walk. One lady further along the road also had two evacuees and on rare occasions - and they were rare - we'd take the children to Morecambe by train for the day. We'd eat our packed sandwiches and then go down to the beach to paddle. I don't think any of us had enough money to go to the fairground.

My parents lived on the outskirts of Kendal and they also had two evacuees, a brother and sister from Tyneside. So, every so often, my two used to go and stay with them. Then at weekends my mother's two kiddies would come and stay with us. This was a treat for the ones who lived with my mother because at that time Kendal had three picture-houses. So all four kiddies could go to the matinee and it was a great change.

It was a very, nice lifestyle. You see, I think the only difference the war made to me was that we were classed as a safety area for evacuees, as I had no-one belonging me to go and fight in the war. The thing was, I treat Joan more like an equal, but when my husband came home for a weekend she sulked all the time. When it came to the Friday when Jack was coming home, Joan would turn to me and say, "Is he coming again?" She was jealous of him and no doubt felt that was she being treat as a child again.

For a long time Joan and Ian's mother didn't write. But one Sunday morning when I was upstairs making the beds, Ian came upstairs very excited, saying, "Oh, me ma's here. She's here in the street." I told him to bring her in and she was a very nice person. Very shy. A coachload of mothers had come from South Shields to see where their children were placed. She was very appreciative, as Joan had been a very nervy and hysterical child, and asked how I coped when "Our Joan threw a hysterical fit and rolled about on the floor". I could only say that Joan never did that with me.

After that, each week or fortnight, a parcel used to come for Joan and Ian from their mother. Inside would be their comics and some sweets and a bar of chocolate for my own son, Gordon. I think people would be paid eight shillings and sixpence for each evacuee they had. Later on the Government decided that parents had to contribute so much towards their children, so the parcels didn't arrive quite so often after that. However, they were an extremely poor family with Mother going out to do daily cleaning, as their father who worked in the shipyards had been laid off quite a lot. But we managed. Their mother used to knit their socks and send them through and I'd darn and patch

their clothes.

We were strictly rationed but we ate good and very plain, nourishing meals. I had a kitchen garden which I kept going, and made stews and a lot of soup with bones. I used to get a full shin bone from the butchers each week and get him to break it into sizes that I could get into my pan. I'd simmer these bones for a day and a night, then the liquid poured from the pan, set [solidified] with about an inch of fat. This fat was the marrow from the bones, which I'd clarify and use to make cakes, gingerbread and some pastries. The stock was so thick it was full of goodness and was cut into cubes which were used as a base for vegetable soup. It wasn't a fancy diet but it was nourishing, and I made my own bread. I was thrifty and nothing was spent on anything unnecessary. In those days, you never bought fruit - at least I didn't. I couldn't afford apples and oranges, you see, and it's difficult to imagine, but even sausage was kept under the butcher's counter.

I had ration books for myself and the three children and we decided not to have sugar in our tea but save the sugar rations for making cakes. So I saved these coupons to the last week in the month and went to the shop where I was registered and asked for my four weeks' rations of sugar. The manager told me I couldn't have it because I'd proved I could go without sugar for a month. Therefore I'd lost all the coupons. I never quite got over that, and every week after, I made sure I got my full ration of everything.

In those days nobody had shampoos for their hair, they just used soap and water. My house didn't have a bathroom, only a long zinc bath that was

FOOD FACTS

Number 31

Every night our stout-hearted lorry drivers are risking their lives to bring you food. They don't let you down—so don't let them down by wasting food.

WHAT do you put in your "carried meal"? Here are a few suggestions for things that are possibly tastier and more digestible than those you make now. These are cheap and hardly any trouble to prepare. Have them at home too, sometimes; they always make a good meal.

ON THE KITCHEN FRONT

Savoury Splits

These are delicious, filling things to have during a day's hard work or a night watch.

Sift 6 ozs. plain flour with 2 level teaspoonfuls baking powder and ¼ teaspoonful salt. Mix thoroughly with 4 ozs. sieved cooked potato (sieved, if possible, when still hot). Rub in 1 oz. fat and blend to a soft dough with 4 tablespoonfuls milk. Roll out to ¼" thickness on a well-floured board and cut into rounds. Glaze the tops with a little milk. Bake in a hot oven for 15 minutes. When cold, split the scones and fill with one of these mixtures.

1. Finely diced cooked vegetables bound with a little white sauce.

2. Finely diced cooked beetroots bound with horseradish or some other sharp sauce.

3. Mixed vegetable curry.

4. Shredded raw cabbage heart well mixed with mayonnaise and chopped parsley.

Sweet Splits

If you like something in the sweet line, make your splits as above,

but for the filling mix some cocoa and sugar (or honey) to a cream with milk. Then work into it a little creamed margarine.

Piccaninnies

These are grand energy givers, and are good to take to work if you are able to heat food there. All you do is to scrub a large potato and bake it in its jacket till soft. Cut in half lengthwise, scoop out the middle and mix with any of these fillings.

1. Equal quantities of cooked shredded cabbage, diced carrot and turnip, bound with white sauce and flavoured with a dash of piquant sauce.

2. Roughly chopped kipper bound with mustard sauce.

3. Shredded winter greens cooked in a very little water with some shreds of bacon, flavoured with salt, pepper and mustard, and bound with enough flour to thicken.

Pile up whichever mixture you choose in one half of the potato jacket, put the other half on top, and press together. Replace in the oven to heat through.

For the Youngsters

Give your child a raw carrot every day. It's a grand thing for children of all ages. It clears the complexion, and helps to build strong teeth and bones

Listen to Freddie Grisewood, the well-known compere, on the Radio Kitchen Front at 8.15 every morning this week.

73

called a bungalow bath. It was a very long bath that hung outside on a nail in the yard. Like everyone else we carted it in on a Friday night, had the kettle boiling, and topped the water up for each person.

We had a wireless but it wasn't part of your life like television is now. The wireless had batteries which we had to take and get charged every so often. As we didn't even get a newspaper or listen to the news, we didn't know about a lot of the hazards or downside of the war.

Adults from other parts of the country were also sent here to help with the war work or as evacuees. A married couple rented a furnished house near me. The wife was always saying to me, could I get this or that for her. Well, I couldn't get anything for myself, never mind for somebody else. However, once I was given six eggs at Easter to make pasche eggs for the children, so I gave this lady three of them. Later a relation of theirs came to see me and told me never to give them anything. He asked if he could go upstairs to my bedroom which overlooked this couple's yard. From the bedroom he pointed out a brand new zinc dolly tub that this lady had in her yard, which was full of eggs. What this couple were doing was going round the farms, buying eggs and selling them to their friends.

Another time I was queuing with a lot of other women at a fishmonger's. We'd queued for hours because we heard there was fish due in the shop. I was behind a lady who had just moved to the area, when the fishmonger brought out this very big, fresh cod. The lady said, "You needn't cut it up, I'll take it as it is." It was wrong of the fishmonger, but he gave her all that fish, which we ordinary housewives couldn't have afforded. So that was that. All the other women and myself had queued for nothing, as that was the last fish. Yes, it was true that locals abided by the rules and others didn't. Perhaps it's a case of sour grapes, but I was never offered anything other than my flat rations. Maybe if I'd been offered, I would have taken it.

Towards the end of the war I had to go into hospital, and Joan and Ian's Mother wouldn't allow her children to stay anywhere else. They could have stayed somewhere on a temporary basis but she was afraid they wouldn't settle, so the children went back home. At about this time my husband was sent to Short's at Windermere where they made the flying boats. That meant he lived at home and travelled daily until after the war finished. So, to be honest, we were really a little unit on our own and the war seemed to pass us by.

When the war finished, oh, it was wonderful. You see, all of us women on the street did our own baking and it was amazing what we made. Most of us had a little bit of something hoarded away and, well, it was no time to hoard any longer. Out it all came. Trestle tables were organised from somewhere and husbands set them up by the side of the houses. And we set all this food out. We had little races and games and then, I'll always remember, as the children, mothers, fathers, relations and everybody was sitting down to eat this feast, a couple passed by - real business people. The woman turned to her husband and said, "Well, you know, these poor children will never had seen food like this in their lives." We all took offence at this because we'd all coped and done very well with our rations.

After the war, Jack continued working at Short's at Windermere, and then the firm closed down. So he was out of work again, for quite a long time, just like before the war. And Joan, I met her again years later. She'd married by that time and was on holiday, camping somewhere on the outskirts of Kendal with her husband, and they came to see me. She did look well, and told me that Ian was in the Merchant Navy. But I've never seen Ian again, and he was such a wonderful, cheery boy, he really was.

Alice, now a widow with grandchildren, still lives in Kendal.

TEN

'Hey, they've just declared war'

∽

Thomas Henry Scott, *born 1923 at Martindale.*

I'd been to Penrith with my father and we were coming home on the bus when Father got talking to this chap. The chap was from Pooley Bridge and said that he wanted a lad for farm work. My father said, "I've one here. He's not doing much." So they struck a bargain for me to go and work at Pooley Bridge. I had nothing to do with it.

My wage for general farm work at Pooley Bridge was fifteen pounds for six months. One Sunday morning I was just walking across the yard when the boss shouts, "Hey, they've just declared war." But at that time we just carried on as normal. Nothing altered for quite a while. Then the following Whitsun, in 1940 I left Pooley Bridge. I went back home to our farm at Martindale and stopped there all winter, working for my dad.

About a year after the war started, a training camp for the army was opened near our farm. The building used was called The Bungalow and had been a stalkers' lodge for deer stalking. This building and one further down the hill were made into an army camp (Battle School) where they sent non-commissioned officers straight out of training college.

The road up to The Bungalow had been just chippings and it had always been said that you couldn't get a wagon up there as it was so steep. But the army tarred the road and went up. They were definitely the first ones that took

DACRE LODGE

MISSIONARY SALE

14th SEPTEMBER, is
CANCELLED.

BROUGH SHOW

listed for THURSDAY, 14th SEPTEM-
BER, 1939, is
CANCELLED.

**THRELKELD
SHEEP DOG TRIALS**

ABANDONED.

SHAP SHOW and SPORTS

SATURDAY, 16th SEPTEMBER,
CANCELLED.

OUSBY AND CULGAITH
AGRICULTURAL SOCIETY.

SHOW, 23rd SEPTEMBER,
has been
CANCELLED.

**NENTHEAD
AGRICULTURAL SHOW**

and HOUND TRAIL
CANCELLED.

wagons up that way. And there wasn't any electricity past Howtown for telephones until the army got up there.

Well, up at Martindale these lads were put through their paces. As part of the training, they were taken down to School Bridge and had to creep up the beck with live ammunition being fired over their heads. These officers were often on night manoeuvres. I've seen them up the valley on a night and tracer bullets and thunder flashes were being used.

As the army camp was near our house, the lads used to come across to my mother's and she used to make them ham and egg teas. They spent a lot of time at our house did some of them lads. Some even come back after the war to have a look round. But at the time it was all hush, hush what they did. Same as when they had the Tank Corps at Lowther Park near Penrith. They had sacking fencing all the way round the place so that nobody could look over. The story goes that some lasses used to knock about with the soldiers from there and finished up in the family way. When they asked who was responsible, the lasses didn't know, as each bloke had a black beret on at the time.

There were a few bombs dropped around Martindale and some at Grisedale, but these were probably dumped by the Germans on their way home. One of our planes (a Lockheed Hudson from Silloth) came down on Beda Fell, behind Dale Head. The police came up to our house and then went on to guard the plane overnight. I was at home at the time, and the next morning I took the air force rescue team up to the crash site. There had been four fellas in the plane but they had all been smashed up with bits here and bits there.

Planes used to fly low over Ullswater Lake from Carlisle way (RAF Kingstown at Carlisle). One fella used to fly up and tip the plane so that he'd touch the water with one wing and then the other. One day he tipped the plane too far over and into the lake he went. He managed to get out but it isn't many years since they managed to get the plane out of the lake.

My father and his mate, Jack Taylor, were Special Constables up Martindale. They were given an armband each, and away they went. This amused me a lot. They used to go out on a night looking for any farm that was showing lights in the blackout. Well, the farms up that way were miles apart. So by the time they got to the farm, the owners could have gone to bed and put the lights out. Father and his mate were supposed to be out on duty two nights a week. Mind, if the weather was wild, they wouldn't go. They'd pick their nights to be out and about. When you think, whoever thought of such an idea? Two Special Constables up Martindale.

After being at home, I went to work at a farm up Hartsop. It was about that time that the War Ag (War Agricultural Committee) came into being.

They came round farms telling everybody what to do. That was rather laughable because in a lot of places half the folk on the War Ag were farmers who had gone bankrupt.

Local Wartime Farming.

RESUMPTION OF BULL LICENSING.

Farm Men for the Forces.

On the outbreak of war the suspension of bull licensing was announced, but the Minister of Agriculture has decided to arrange for the resumption of licensing in order that the progress which has so far been achieved should be maintained, and to prevent any deterioration in the standard of cattle. To effect economy in expenditure on staff and to save the time of farmers in complying with their obligations under the Act, certain simplifications in procedure will be introduced.

TRUSTING THE MAN ON THE SPOT.

The permission for the County War Agricultural Committees to use their discretion in recommending roots, kale and other green crops as suitable crops to be grown in certain instances on newly ploughed up grassland is important. Many cases have been brought to the notice of the Ministry where it would be obviously more sensible for roots to be grown on the newly ploughed land, and corn grown on existing arable, rather than to risk a corn crop where wireworms are rampant.

FARM MEN FOR THE FORCES.

Farmers are reminded that, although all men within the age group 20 to 22 will have to register, the only men to be called up from agriculture will be those who are now 20 years old and younger men as they attain that age. The Schedule reserves farmers and most classes of farm workers at the age of 21 years. Men registered this year under the Military Training Act who have since attained the age of 21 years will not be called up, and none of this year's class will be called up until November. So far as can be foreseen, the annual loss to agriculture in future years will be not more than about 15,000 men, or some 3 per cent. of the wage-earning men and boys regularly employed in farming,

The farm I was at had two young lads, evacuees from Newcastle. They'd never been in the country before and hadn't a clue. One day they were playing in a field when one of them started crying. He said the grass was biting him. It was the nettles stinging and I had to tell him to move out of them. It was very seldom that their mother could come across from Newcastle to see them, but when she came she'd stop overnight. You see, the transport was shocking really. There was very few buses and petrol was rationed.

That was a grand lark, was petrol rationing. All these tractors run off coloured petrol and there was plenty of it about. So lads started putting coloured petrol in their cars but if they were caught, they were for it. They got done.

Now cars weren't supposed to be run for pleasure, only business. But there was one lad up Patterdale and he was courting a lass at Pooley Bridge. He always put a sheep in the back seat of his car so if he was stopped he could say he was on farm business. This old sheep used to get in and out of the car itself, it had been in that often.

It was while I was at Hartsop I joined the Home Guard at Patterdale Village Hall next door to the school. There was about twenty of us in the Home Guard, mostly farm lads and one or two who worked at the Greenside lead mines. Four of us at a time would do night duty in the Village Hall. If we were needed, it was the schoolmaster next door who would be phoned, as he was the only one with a telephone. He had to take the message and come and inform us what it was.

We did one or two Sunday afternoon manoeuvres in the Home Guard.

They put us up against the army and we had no chance. "Bang, you're dead." We were dead before we realised the army was there. It was a real laugh. It also amused me, going on guard duty with empty rifles when the army lads were sitting in the Ullswater Hotel or in the White Lion having a drink.

I'd be up at Hartsop for just over a year when I went to the hirings at Penrith and got taken on at a farm at Armathwaite, near Carlisle. Now, Armathwaite was different altogether as there's a lot of ploughing land between Penrith and Carlisle. And the farm was much bigger, with a married man and two farm lads, besides myself. So we did plenty of ploughing for potatoes and corn. When we started digging the taties up, a fella used to come and collect them every day. Most of the potatoes went to fish-and-chip shops at Carlisle.

In the Home Guard at Armathwaite we used to meet and do rifle practice. Then we'd be sent out on guard duty with empty rifles as there was still no ammunition. We were supposed to be guarding the bridge over the River Eden in case the Germans invaded and blew it up.

We had a captain from another Home Guard come to inspect us at Armathwaite. He told us we

had to guard a certain road and "You'll have to drop a tree across the road if you see some (German) tanks coming." Somebody asked, "How the hell do we drop a tree across the road? If the tanks are coming yonder, we wouldn't have time." "Oh," answered the captain, "You'll have to have it sawn half-way through for a start." That was the kind of thing they came out with. Absolute ridiculous. I often think what a load of rubbish it was. Talk about '*Dad's Army*' on television, that wasn't in it.

Tramps seemed to disappear during the war. But one tramp used to come to the farm at Armathwaite at about October time. He'd come for years and looked after the sheep all winter. Come Spring, he'd be off to the Grand National at Liverpool. He told me that he'd been going to the Grand National for over forty years. I asked him, "What do you do all Summer?" "Well, he said, "I'll tell you what it is me lad. It's a poor street in Liverpool that you can't get sixpence out of." So he'd trail round as a tramp in summer and sleep rough. But he'd be back at Armathwaite in winter where it was warm.

I used to like moving around, and after six months I went to Penrith again to be hired. This time I went up Blencarn way, right at the bottom of Cross Fell, and was back among the sheep. After six months up Blencarn way, I was at Penrith Hirings and got taken on at Burneside Hall, near Kendal. That was like going abroad as it took me all day to get there. I walked the three miles from our house up Martindale. Then cadged a lift into Penrith. Caught the bus from Penrith to Kendal and another one to Burneside.

There was a few of us worked at Burneside Hall. A horseman, shepherd, general lad and I was the cowman. Inside the farmhouse was a maid and a housekeeper. I wasn't in the Home Guard there, and to be honest, I don't know how I got out of it. But I did have to go for my medical at Kendal. I passed, A1 and the Officer in Charge said, "Right, Scott, you're A1. You'll get your calling-up papers next week." I'm still waiting for these papers.

With it being near the end of the war, we had German and Italian prisoners-of-war working for us at Burneside Hall. Oh, the Germans were better workers, but they were more arrogant than the Eyeties. Having said that, the two Germans who worked and lived-in on my father's farm were no problem. They were two good lads and one came back not so long since for a visit.

Some Eyeties come to work at Burneside for a few days and were setting (sowing) potatoes. There was one and I couldn't weigh him up. Anyway, he was setting taties too far apart and the boss came and saw what he was doing. So the boss said to this Eyetie,"Nearer together, man. Nearer together." But all the boss got out of the Eyetie was "No comprehend. No comprehend." Eventually the boss turned to me and said, "Show him what I mean," and walked away. When the boss had gone, this Eyetie turned to me, saying, "Bugger him. I might have to come back and pick these." He could talk English as well as I could. We had many a laugh about it as that same lad was sent in the back end (Autumn) to pick taties. As soon as he saw me, he said, "I knew I'd have to come back."

After Burneside, I went up to Penrith Hirings and was taken on at a farm near Crosby Ravensworth. There was quite a lot of ploughing there for me and another young lad from Shap. But when the war finished, I stayed in farming for a while, then got work away from the land.

Now it's all changed for farm lads. During the war, when you went to a farm, you took your ration book with you and gave it to the farmer's wife who fed you. At some places you were well fed and some you weren't. One place it was beans, beans and more beans. I hate baked beans, but we had them morning, noon and night. At another farm, I was given porridge and bread and cheese for breakfast. The boss used to have bacon and eggs. His missus said to me, "He doesn't like porridge so he has bacon and eggs."

With there being more work during the war years, we put in longer hours. But most of the bosses made sure you got up on time every morning. One had a bell in the farm lads' bedroom, which was attached to string through to his bedroom. So as soon as he woke up in the morning, he pulled this string and that set the bell off. Us farm lads used to wrap a stocking round the bell. Then the boss used to come into our bedroom in the morning and play hell when we hadn't got up.

Of course, there was a lot of black market going on. Owners of a well-known hotel used to bike up to my mother's every week to buy bacon and eggs. I can't swear to it but there was a tale going round about a farmer butching a pig that he shouldn't have. Well, the farmer saw the police on their way to his place the next day. So when they arrived to search the farmhouse, matey said, "The wife's in bed, she's not so well." The old lass had been put to bed and the pig shoved in beside her until the police had gone. There was all kinds of tricks went on. The local bobbies got their eggs and didn't bother after that. It was just a case of surviving. Folk butched a sheep or whatever they had. We always had ham hanging up at home. Always had.

I was in the Home Guard at all the places I worked, except Burneside. I think just about all Home Guards were much the same and we were just there in case of invasion. You'd do a bit of drill and were told what to do if the Germans came. I tell you, it was rubbish because we didn't have the ammunition. So what could you do? Nothing. I think you were supposed to hit the Germans over the head with your rifle. The country was in dire straits. We were down and out with nothing to fight with. Churchill (Prime Minister) bluffed the Germans. He really did bluff them, and it was a good job for us that he did.

Mr & Mrs Scott
enjoying retirement

After the war, Thomas worked at a paper mill, auction market and dairy before retiring. Married with a family, Thomas lives in Kendal.

ELEVEN

'Oh, Mother was in a state'

∞

Margaret Potter, born at Crook in 1932.

SOUVENIR
of
1940

COPYRIGHT XPDOGRAPH

Margaret aged 8

I can't really remember war breaking out, but as the years went by, you realised what was going on. You see, we heard about it all at school. We learnt by reading the newspapers and knowing where the different armies were and things like that.

I can remember my gas mask and can still smell it. I thought it was horrible. Little kiddies had these gas masks which had Mickey Mouse things on – a floppy nose and big ears. Oh, I don't think I could have worn one, except for practice, as I can't do with anything over my face - never could. We had to carry these gas masks in a cardboard box along with our sandwiches to school every day. The girls weren't so bad, but the boys used to fight with these boxes and burst them open.

We had lots of evacuees and they filled the school. Crook school had two decent rooms, but with all the evacuees, the older end of us had to be taught in the village hall. One of the evacuee teachers, Miss Frost, taught us in the hall, and we played some awful tricks on her. A few of us girls locked ourselves in the ladies' room and wouldn't come out for her.

The evacuees stayed at the farms round about. They weren't bad at all really and we all mixed in. We were told they were coming and had to help them out because a lot of them were from big towns like Barrow, and some hadn't a clue what the country was like. I remember that there were twins, two little girls, and they couldn't understand that milk came from a cow. Their milk had always come from bottles.

My parents didn't have any evacuees as Mother fostered children. During the war years, she had a little boy and girl. Our house only had two bedrooms but my parents' bedroom was L-shaped, so the little lad slept in a bed of his own in their room. Then in the other bedroom, my sister and me shared a bed and the little girl had one of her own. There was no problems and we went to school together.

On the way to school, we used to meet the troops with their bren-carriers who were staying near the Wild Boar Hotel at Crook. Usually we met them on the road to school, when they were marching to someone's house for their morning coffee. Later on in the day, the troops would go back and forward, sort of practising really.

We didn't have to knit for troops but we had to collect waste paper for the war effort. Old books and magazines and things like that, and take them to school. Once you started collecting waste paper, you got a certificate which said you had the rank of a Private. I worked up to be a Field Marshal and got a cardboard badge. That's gone now, but I still have the certificate. In fact, the school got

RURAL DISTRICT OF SOUTH WESTMORLAND.

Certificate of Merit

awarded by the South Westmorland Rural District Council to

Margaret Gosden,

of .... Main Gap, Crook. .... Age 11 years.

as a token of appreciation for a very valuable contribution to the war effort by collecting over 250 books and magazines during the "Westmorland County Book Recovery Drive," 29th April to 13th May, 1944, and thereby attaining the rank of "Field Marshal" in the Book Recovery Army.

Passed under the Common Seal of the Council this .... day
of .... in the presence of

.... Chairman.

.... Clerk.

a citation and photograph from the King for the effort we put in and the photo was hung up on the school wall.

One morning we went to school and wondered what on earth was in the school yard. It was a barrage balloon from Barrow that had burst and come down. These balloons were used at Barrow shipyard to stop planes coming in low. We could hear the planes at night, but the worst time was when Cooper House at Selside was bombed. When that got hit, we felt the reaction of the bomb at Crook. It sounds daft but Crook is a rocky area and we definitely felt the blast.

It was through the war that we started having school dinners made for us. These were made in the kitchen at the Village Hall. Mrs Reid was the first cook and some of the older girls used to go across to the hall and help her. When dinners started, we were allowed either two helpings of the main course and one helping of pudding or one of the main course and two of pudding. But you see, with the girls helping out, they would see what the pudding was that day and tell the rest of us. So of course if it was a nice pud, we would have one main course and two puds. The staff got wise to that trick.

The first school dinner we had was potatoes, vegetables, steamed fish and parsley sauce. Half the kids didn't like it so we didn't have it again. Still, we were lucky with Mrs Reid as she was a good cook, she really was.

Mr Atkinson from Crook used to bring milk to school in a can, which we'd drink at morning break. However, in cold weather, the little ones had milk and the older ones had chocolate milk. As far as I know, it was a mixture of milk powder and chocolate powder, which you poured hot water onto, to make a drink. You can't get it today but it was the kind of stuff you could eat by the spoonful. It was smashing.

Some of the older lads who'd been at Crook School were in the forces. One lad, Ronald was in the Merchant Navy. Miss Hodgson, our teacher, wasn't very big and he'd been the boss of her before he left school. She would keep him in school for doing something wrong and every time she was looking the other way, he'd move back a seat until he was out the door. He was some lad, was Ronald. Derek Reid, his elder brother, was a pilot and went down in the war. We had a memorial service for him in Crook Church.

The war didn't make much difference at home as we had a small-holding. Dad grew vegetables and Mother had hens and at winter time, we had just enough room for four cows. We 'wintered' them for a chap up Longsleddale and he always sent one that we could milk. Mother used to milk it and keep the cream to make butter. We kept a pig and it got butched, so I suppose that was black market when you think about it, but a lot of people did the same. My mam and dad helped the farmers on each side with their hay. But people thought nothing of helping each other, we all just got on with it.

The breadvan came round Crook once a week, but Mother made most of our bread. We didn't have many hens and the ones we had were just for our own use and a few people round about. Any spare eggs were potted in water-glass for use in winter when the hens weren't laying. These were used for baking as they had to be cracked open in case any had 'gone off'. So they were no use for boiling. I know, when eggs were in short supply, my dad and Uncle Harry went looking for gulls' eggs. But there were dried eggs which were good for making scrambled eggs.

One year Mother got some geese to fatten up for Christmas. Come Christmas week and the geese flew away. Oh, Mother was in a state, but Dad said, "Never mind, they'll come back." He was right, because about four days later, the geese flew back and Mother killed them in time for Christmas. We also kept guinea-fowl, and squawking things they were. The little beggars used to lay all over the place and we could never find their eggs.

Haytime at Crook
during the war years

There must have been eight or ten damson trees in our garden. We'd pluck the damsons and put a score of them at a time in big rounds (baskets). Tommy Walling from Crosthwaite used to come and collect them and I think they'd be taken to Kendal market. The only other fruit that I remember we could get were apricots and prunes. I got sick of them, and for years after, I couldn't stand them. We never had ice-cream, and the first I would have had, was from Tognarelli's at Kendal after the war. It was the best ice-cream I ever tasted.

At home we used to have rabbit pie and crow pie. You could soon catch a rabbit by setting a snare. Then my sister and me would go with Dad to get some crows at the rookery, which was quite near. As crows can't count, Dorothy and me would walk away and leave Dad there to pot off (shoot) the young ones who perched on the branches while learning how to fly. They were easy prey.

As children we had to help out with the work. We fed the hens and pig and carried water from the spring. No, there was no inside water, it was a spring that had been levelled into a big metal well. It was grand, fresh water. Once a year we'd empty the well, clean and whitewash it all out, let it dry and fill up again.

At nights, we used to listen to the radio. Tommy Handley in *I.T.M.A* (*It's That Man Again*). That was good, and we always listened to him. You see, nobody had television in them days. But one chap, I think he delivered the post and was a conscientious objector, he used to tell us that the day would come when we would sit in our living room and watch pictures in a box. Well, we didn't believe him.

My dad was exempt from the forces as he worked as a linesman for the Manchester Corporation Water Works. As he worked on the stretch of pipeline between Longsleddale and Kendal, he had a motor-bike and side-car to get to work. He kept all his gear for the bike in an old stable we had. One night when my sister and me were lying in bed, I could see all this light. Then after a bit, there was such a carry-on. Dad had been soldering some part of the motor-bike, set fire to the bench and there was flames everywhere. My mother went hairless as it was the blackout, you see. So there they both were, running up and down from the well with buckets, trying to douche this fire. Oh dear, poor Dad. He wasn't very popular over that.

With living at home, Dad was a sergeant in the Home Guard and out on duty at night. One of the ladies nearby, whose husband was also in the Home Guard, wouldn't stay in the house on her own. I wasn't that old and I had to go and sleep with her. I didn't like that as it was a three-storey house and she had us sleeping right at the top.

It was about 1944 that we moved from Crook to Longsleddale, as it was nearer Dad's work. I know there'd been some right bad winters during the war and Dad and his mate who worked together were stranded up at the (water) strainer house at the top of Longsleddale for a week or maybe a fortnight. It depended on the weather and how deep the snow was. But they had heating and food with them and didn't come to any harm.

When we moved from Crook, I attended Longsleddale school, which had only one room, but quite a few children attended. I know when the war finished we went back to Crook for the celebrations and Dad was in charge of the fireworks.

I wasn't quite fourteen when I left school in 1946. You see, you could get a work card and leave school at fourteen. You didn't get a chance to stay on then, did you? You did what you were told. I went into farm service where the Mr and Mrs had six children and two men helping on the farm.

Even though this was after the war, we still had prisoners-of-war helping in the summer time. There were Germans and Italians and one time we had an Irish lad. One German we had, when he came in for his tea and got talking, he told us that if he had a gun he'd kill us. AND he meant it. He was a real Nazi. Now the Italians were different again. They were all right, were the Italians. My future husband was showing one Italian how to plant potatoes and asked him what his job had been before the war. Do you know what he'd been? A waiter on a train. So planting potatoes would be a real change for him.

It was living-in work on the farm, and I'd start at half-past six in the morning and finish when I finished. It was a great big house to scrub and I worked outside as well. We had animals to feed and many a time we had sixteen calves to feed in the morning. Then I washed up in the dairy. We used a big old-fashioned boiler in the back kitchen with a fire underneath it, that we'd fill up for washing day. Oh, it was hard work, was all that, and all for ten shillings a week.

Margaret was in farm service until marriage, when she became a farmer's wife and had six children. Now a widow, Margaret lives at Orton.

TWELVE

'Away John, on the shore'

*John Stobbart, born 1929 at Workington and living at Salterbeck estate at the outbreak of war. **Edith** Stobbart [wife], born 1932 at Salterbeck.*

JOHN: We didn't have an Anderson shelter in our house but Mr Murphy next door did. When the bomb fell on Poole Road near where we lived, me and a young lass called Annie were frying some bacon over the open fire at home. As soon as I heard that bomb drop, it was bugger the bacon and bugger Annie, she could look after herself. I nearly knocked Mr Murphy out of the way running into his Anderson shelter.

Greyhound Racing

AT

LONSDALE PARK, WORKINGTON
EVERY SATURDAY
AT 3-30

EDITH: I can remember the sirens going. Now this was before we had an Anderson shelter, and my dad pushed all us kids into the outside coal-house. When our Anderson shelter did eventually come, we used that as a table. It stood right underneath the window with a bit of oil cloth on top instead of a table cloth.

JOHN: Before the war my dad was just labouring on the docks or got odd (occasional) shifts on the steelworks. But during the war he was working full time on the floating plant. That was on the dredger, tug-boat, and two hoppers. The tug-boat pulled the dredger to where all the silt was near the harbour. Then the dredger brought up all the silt and muck from the seabed and loaded it onto a hopper. Finally, the hopper took the muck away and dumped it out at sea. So with Dad doing this work, he got seamen's rations and a cigarette allowance. He was classed as a seaman with having to keep the port clear for the ammunition boats coming in.

Besides ammunition boats, there was all sorts of other boats come into the harbour to unload. I know a boat used to come in with boxes of tea. A box would get 'accidentally' knocked and burst open. So Dad stuffed all this loose tea down his trousers, which were tied around the ankles, so it wouldn't drop out. That's how he brought tea home. And he wasn't the only one. But the ordinary public wasn't allowed onto the docks and there was always the police or army wandering about.

EDITH: Well a brother-in-law of mine managed to get on the docks and swopped a man's suit that he had for a big bag of rice from one of the foreign seamen. My sister had all this rice in a bath, washing it, because there was weevils in it.

My dad worked on the steelworks during the war so we always had firewood that was brought off the works in his bait box. It wasn't until I was grown-up that I saw people rolling newspapers up and then twisting it to start a fire. You see, we'd always used the wood dad had brought home in his bait box to light a fire in the mornings.

It was the gantry where Dad worked. That was just a railway line on stilts where railway wagons tipped spoil from the pits into the sea. Then the sea would disperse the spoil. Dad would be waiting for a wagon to come and then sort among the spoil for coal. He would have said to Mam, "Send the kids down," and we'd go down to the gantry with a pram, fill it with coal and push it home. That was a killer, pushing a pram full of coal up a steep hill round here.

JOHN: The sea would separate the heavy from the light spoil. And the light stuff was coal that would wash back up onto the shore. Folk would go onto the shore with anything with wheels on. Prams, bikes or bogies built with pram wheels. I've known people take a babby's (baby's) pram down onto the shore for coal. When the coal was taken home, the pram would be washed out and the babby put back into the pram.

One day a twenty-ton railway wagon was shunted by mistake onto the shore and left there. Well, there was bloody great lumps of coal on this wagon. So I was on top of it, chucking all the best bits of coal onto the ground, ready to try and take home. I looked over the side of the wagon and there was 'Nabber' Walton, the Mossbay bobby, watching me. "Nice coal, eh, John? Now get the bloody lot put back," he shouted. The wagon was too big to chuck the coal back into. It had ladders up the back end. So I had to climb up and down these ladders with every bloody bit of coal until it was all put back. When I got home I was black as the ace of spades. I dare'nt tell my mam what had happened. But I used to get up to all bloody sorts, and each time 'Nabber' Walton would appear and say, "You needn't run, John. I know where you live." And he did.

Aerial photograph of Workington Iron & Steel Company 1935

EDITH: 'Nabber' Walton lived on Mossbay hill. You can still see the marks were the police crest was on the outside of the house. The policemen lived in ordinary houses that had the constabulary crest on them. But 'Nabber' was a grand fella. It's only as you get older than you realise how grand.

JOHN: All the Ropery leading onto the shore had barbed wire in case of invasion and most of the railway arches along by the shore were sealed off for the same reason. You weren't stopped going on and off the shore. It was just to slow down any invading troops. On the Ropery was an army camp which had two machine-gun nests. One was on top of the Ropery hill, and the other, on top of the slag bank.

At the time there was a lot of talk on the wireless about Fifth Columnists. You know, infiltrators. So me and my mate were pretending to be these Fifth Columnists. On top of the slag bank was two big mounds that we called 'the Tits' where the machine-gun nest was. It was very steep getting up to 'the Tits but, living round here, we could manage it no bother. We scraffled up to where the Lewis guns were and pinched all the bullets.

Two magazines full of bullets. When we got down off the slag bank, we started dropping bricks onto the magazines to see what would happen. That's kids, isn't it? Anyway, we left the magazines on the ground because the military police were looking for them.

My dad was in the Home Guard and came home one day from training with a wooden rifle. I was still pretending to be a Fifth Columnist and start playing with this wooden rifle, which was as big as me. I got a good hiding for that.

The Home Guard used to practise on the shore. One time, the proper army people came to show them how to fire a phosphorus bomb from a mortar. Well, the bomb hit a rock and the rock burst into flames. Even the Home Guard ran. It was bloody terrifying. When the tide came in, it put the phosphorus out. But when the tide went out, the phosphorus lit itself again.

My dad didn't go out much with the Home Guard because he was on tide work, you see. six hours on and six hours off. And my mam didn't go out to work. I think she had her hands full with me.

*C.1940 at Salterbeck. The photograph, nicknamed
The Three Stooges, shows Edith (centre)
with two of her sisters, Betty (left) and Lena (right)*

EDITH: Married women didn't go out to work then. It was really only when women went into munitions and other jobs for the war effort that they started working. During the war my mam had four cleaning jobs in the mornings and went from one to another. Besides that she was taking in washing. Our mangle used to stand in the bathroom and my mam would put a sheet in one end, and you'd be standing holding and pulling the sheet as it came out the other end to get it straight.

When you think back, our parents must have had a hell of a life. They used to barter a lot during the war years. If anybody had any spare sugar, they would swoop it for butter. Then our mothers would go to a rummage sale and try to get a cardigan. It would be washed, unravelled and knitted up again. They were always doing things like that, and prodding mats.

With Mam being so busy, us kids would go and queue at the shops for her. You'd queue at a cake shop and get four cakes. You'd queue at another shop for pies. When you'd finished, you'd go and have a cup of tea at Woollies (Woolworth's) as it had a little tea counter in them days. But I remember queuing for a rabbit. And at teatime us kids would be sitting at the table and Dad would be dishing the food out. Now, there's only two kidneys in a rabbit and we'd be sitting waiting to see whose plate dad was going to put the kidney on. There was nine of us kids and we all wanted a kidney.

Everybody turned their gardens over for produce. Where the cemetery is now, there was allotments and a big static water tank, which was the fire point. Like other places, Salterbeck had parlour shops. These were usually just little sweet shops in people's parlours. Piper Elliot had one on Shore Road, Mrs Routledge on Wetheriggs Road and Mrs Braithwate on Jackson Road. Also we had a local woman, Mrs McIlroy, whose son was a prisoner-of-war come round for Tommy Smokes Fund. People would give money for cigarettes to be sent to our troops.

CIGARETTES FOR OUR SOLDIERS, SAILORS, AND AIRMEN OVERSEAS

"West Cumberland Times" SMOKES FUND

Subscribers Invited To Name Relatives And Friends

Arrangements With Famous Tobacco Firm For Export Of Parcels Free Of Duty

JOHN: A neighbour used to come and knock on our door and say, "Away John, on the shore. Let's see what's going on." That was when the tide was coming in, because some queer stuff came up with the tide. Just a couple of years after the war started, there'd been a lot of boats getting torpedoed in the Irish Sea. So instead of lifeboats they had wooden rafts which had a big tank in the centre, filled with emergency rations. If a boat was sunk, these rafts floated off. They were eventually washed up on the shore and we used to get the rations. There'd be cigarettes, chocolate and fishing lines. Mind, those neighbour would whip (quickly take) the cigarettes and I'd get the fishing line.

Then there'd be smashed up lifeboats and ships' masts coming onto the shore. This neighbour made a bloody big greenhouse with wood off the shore. It was all good wood and made a fine, big greenhouse. Once we found twenty-eight pound of butter. It was all in boxes and the top of the butter had a thin layer of gravel on it, but we just cut that off and used all the rest.

EDITH: Can you remember, they even took the name-plates down at the railway stations during the war. And most of the cars were taken off the road. In fact, the only person I ever knew who had a car was the insurance man. But his car was off the road during the war because there was hardly any petrol. At night-time, when we were on a bus, everything was pitch black. The shout used to be, "Where are we at?" as you really didn't know where you were.

Of course, in the blackout, kids could get up to all sorts of mischief. One lad used to take our garden gate off, then knock on the front door. Somebody would run out after him and fall over the gate in the dark. This lad used to boast that my father couldn't catch him. Little did he know that he was going to go to my father a few years later and ask for his daughter's had in marriage. He's now my brother-in-law.

JOHN: I played a lot on the reservoir right behind our house. One day in the middle of winter we were playing there on the ice. This evacuee from down south came to play and we thought she spoke posh. Well, she was posh, because she had skates on and we were in our clogs. We couldn't afford skates so I suppose she was showing off a little bit. I said to her, "I bet you can't skate over there and touch that rose." Well, this metal rose was for cooling the water in the reservoir from the

CONDITION OF EVACUEES.

Complaints at County P.A.C. Meeting.

Complaints that children who had arrived in Cumberland as evacuees were poorly clad were made at a meeting of the Cumberland Public Assistance Committee held at Carlisle yesterday afternoon.

Mr. J. W. Gilbertson, Maryport, asked if the Public Assistance Committee could do anything towards rigging these children out.

The Chairman (Mr. W. Johnston, Penrith)—We have nothing to do with it. Newcastle and other places are responsible. Why should we shoulder the responsibility?

Father Clayton, Cleator, said some of the children had come poorly clad, some without footwear, and some without stockings. Was it the responsibility of the Public Assistance Committee or the Education Committee?

The Clerk (Mr. Allan Hodgson)—It is the duty of Newcastle.

Mr. J. Douglas, Aspatria, declared that many of the parents of the evacuees were earning good money, so how could it be the responsibility of the Public Assistance Committee of Newcastle? "Some of these children," he declared, "are a disgrace to civilisation. It is not the fault of the children but of the parents."

The Public Assistance Officer (Mr. C. W. Walker) said he was in communication with the Government Department on this and other problems, and he hoped the Committee would leave it to the officials to act on information received from the Government.

This the Committee agreed to do.

steelworks. And the nearer you got to the rose, the thinner the ice was. Off she skated across to the rose and plopped in the water. We were cruel because everybody started laughing. And the worst thing was, we were going to take her skates and use them ourselves but she lost one in the water. That lass never came back to play with us. She was an evacuee staying at Mossbay.

EDITH: We got our gas masks at Mossbay School. I think all of Salterbeck must have gone there to get them. Occasionally when you were at school the teachers would say, "You're leaving here at such and such a time. Check the time when you get home to see how long it's taken you." That was to see how long it took kids to get home in case there was an invasion or emergency.

In them days, when you were eleven, you sat your exams. The clever ones got to the Grammar School, which took boys and girls, but they were separated. Both me and my sister Lena got into Central School. I think I just scraped through. After that it was either Victoria School for the girls or Guard Street for the boys. But you always went to school. If you weren't at school, the School-board Men, Mr Stockdale and Mr Stephenson, used to come looking for you on their bikes. It was an awful thing, a shaming, if the School-board Man came to anybody's house.

JOHN: I went to Guard Street School and you just had the same teacher right through school, except for music lessons. Oh, the teacher I had, he could chuck blackboard erasers round bloody corners. If there was twenty-seven other kids and he aimed for you, he would hit you. Well, he always hit me, anyway.

When I was fourteen I found myself a job. You could pack one job in and go and get another one the next day as there was so much work here during the war. I went onto the steelworks, and there were so many men missing with going to war that women were doing men's jobs. Steel workers weren't deferred, that's why women were working there.

Oh, they came from all over to work at the steelworks. They used to put special buses on to bring workers in from outlying districts. That continued for years and years. I can remember local men walking to work in droves. A horn (siren) used to sound at six in a morning, two in the afternoon and at ten at night. This was for the shift change-overs and could be heard all over the town.

I was working on the sleeping mills, feeding plates into the furnace. Oh, it was a hot job, but it was day work as the furnace closed down at night because of the blackout. I think it would be half past seven in the morning

95

till four in the afternoon that I worked. I was supposed to give my mam all my wages. Let's put it this way, she never got it all.

I'd take bread and jam to work for my bait (snack) but got a cup of tea at the canteen. There was always larl (little) bait cabins dotted all over the steelworks. Larl cabins that blokes sat in, out of the way. Inside the cabin was a round stove with a ring of bottles round it. Maybe old wine bottles or something like that, for folk to heat their tea in. But if you went as a stranger, you couldn't put your bottle in any particular place, because it belonged to somebody else. And you couldn't sit on just any seat, as you'd be told, "That's so-and-so's seat. It was the same with shovels. "Don't touch that one. It belongs to so-and-so."

I was working on the steelworks when the war finished. Believe it or not, I didn't smoke or drink then. And the only dance I went to, I wore a pair of cut-down wellies. I stayed at the steelworks until 1948 when I left to do my National Service.

John & Edith
1995

John was a factory worker until retirement, while Edith was in service,
then a factory worker until their marriage. They are still living at
Salterbeck and are now grandparents.

THIRTEEN

'All sorts of dodges we'd get up to'

Geoff Carradus, *born 1927 at Kirkbarrow, Kendal.*

One of my elder brothers, Jimmy, was a big Territorial man. He was a sergeant and doing a recruitment drive prior to war breaking out. Well, he got Albert, another brother, to join, and while they were at the TA camp near Lancaster, war was declared. They never came back home. They were drafted right away up to Carlisle and that's when they were drilling with broomhandles and all this carry-on, as there was no rifles or uniforms for them.

Geoff's brother, Albert (left) and Charley
'Jock' Milton (right) Both were part of the British
Expeditionary Force (1940)

Albert went with the Expeditionary Force to France. I can remember the 4th Border Regiment standing on the forecourt of Kendal Railway Station. Most of them never came back or were taken prisoner. Albert was a dispatch driver and he managed to get on board ship and come back. You see, the '4th Borders' was the local regiment and most of the lads were in it from the early

Part of the Expeditionary Force,
on the forecourt of Kendal Railway Station

days at the start of the war. Some lads who were fifteen gave their wrong ages and joined up. One of my pals joined and was actually in France when they found out his proper age and sent home back home again.

I went to the old Dean Gibson School at Kendal. Even though it was a Catholic School, it took Protestants. I'm not a Catholic but we lived so handy to the school. Only across the road, you see. All these evacuees came to school from Newcastle and South Shields. We couldn't take any of them at home, as we lived in a very small house and there was eight of us. These evacuees used the school for half a day and us locals used it for the other half. When they were at school, we used temporary premises or went on nature walks. Or was supposed to, but we dispersed. You know, played hooky.

There was quite a lot of upheaval at the time and adults, mostly from Newcastle way, came to Kendal. There was also troops based round here and a NAFFI was set up above the premises of Burton's, the tailors. I remember going up there. It was just one big room where you could get a snack and a cup of tea.

When you left school at fourteen, you were left to your own devices to get a job. I went to work at the Lakeland Laundry on Shap Road as a van boy. There was no washing machines in them days, so most folk's washing came to the laundry. The laundry vans used to go around collecting dirty washing and delivering the clean stuff. Funnily enough, the troops' laundry wasn't done at the Kendal branch but went up to Carlisle. There would be about ten to twelve laundry vans. Obviously they were rationed for petrol, but that was in the early years of the war and rationing wasn't so acute then.

I came off the vans and went inside the laundry to work. I think I worked on practically every job there. Where they used to bring the laundry in, was called 'the dumping'. I used to sent the washing up to girls who sorted it out. From there it was sent down to washers, then on to the packaging end. I had to put the packages into various racks in the garage. Each van had its own run, and they took the laundry out on their next day's delivery.

It was a sweatshop was that place. I always said that I'd never send my worst enemy to work there. I think we'd work from eight in the morning till six at night during the week and till midday on a Saturday. My wage was fifteen shillings a week and I gave it to my mother. I used to get back two bob a week pocket money. But two bob was a lot of money in them days and you could do a lot with it.

Well, at fifteen we were drinking like they do nowadays. If we had any money left at weekends, there might be a cheap trip to Morecambe, which was about one shilling return. You could go on these special trips from Kendal Railway Station, which included entrance to the Winter Gardens. You'd see an old-time variety show, and from there to the ballroom for a dance. It was all included in the price. I always remember we used to go down into a cellar part of the Winter Gardens, which was called the Parisian Bar. A gang of us would go, and we'd be drinking and scratch our names on these marble-topped tables. We were only fifteen at the time and it didn't take much to make us drunk and we used to get really legless.

After working at the laundry for about a year, I went to work with my eldest brother at Schweppes soft drinks depot on the Lound at Kendal. They had only one lorry, a three-ton Morris Commercial. We'd put a load of soft drinks onto the lorry as we had an idea what our customers wanted. Then off we'd go round our area, maybe Grange-Over-Sands one day and Barrow another day. We'd call at the hotels and sell the drinks off the vehicle. There was no cash, as it was all bills that were sent later on to the customers. That was the method in those days, you sold off the vehicle. But Schweppes only supplied big, posh hotels. There was none of this selling to corner shops.

We sold soft drinks and the special one was tonic, which Schweppes was famous for. The others were ginger beer, siphons of soda, and the normal cordials of lemon squash and orange squash. Every bottle was individually wrapped in tissue paper and beautifully packed. Of course we had our special calls, where you'd be asked to go in for a drink or a cup of tea and get a sandwich.

We were on the Grange-Over-Sands run when some incendiaries were dropped at Allithwaite. I saw the three end houses with their roofs burnt out. And Barrow, we were delivering there after one of the heavy bombing raids. As you go down Abbey Road, there's a big church down the right-hand side. On the opposite side, on the corner was the Trevelyan Hotel. Well, an aerial torpedo came right through the apex of the church roof, then straight through the roof and hit the corner of this hotel. Just absolutely flattened it.

On our travels for Schweppes we saw a lot of troop movement. As the war developed, a lot of hotels in the Lakes area were taken over by the army. Such as the Prince of Wales Hotel in Grasmere, that was taken over for a training unit for bren carriers. Kendal was a busy town as it was on the main road through to Scotland. All traffic had to come through Kendal. I can remember when the Americans first came through as they were blasé and throwing their money around. Us kids used to stand on Netherfield Bridge and as these American convoys passed, they'd throw money at us. And land wagons called Queen Mary's were used to cart aeroplanes about that had crashed. These Queen Mary's used to park up on New Road at Kendal overnight with wrecked German planes on them. As lads we used to go and raid them for souvenirs.

Schweppes didn't last very long because restrictions came in for the soft drinks industry. The Government brought in an order that the areas were all going to be zoned and a local firm called Alexander's was given this area to cover. So Schweppes had to close its depot. Well, at the same time my brother who I worked with was called up for war work as he was too old for the forces. I was still only fifteen and had to close the Schweppes depot down and get rid of all the stock. I was sent packing cases to put all the bottles of pop in them. These were sent by rail and sold off to the County Hotel and Crown and Mitre up at Carlisle. Then the depot was filled to the gunnel with empty egg-boxes. Thousands and thousands of them. The depot was being used as a store because no crates were being manufactured and egg-boxes were being used instead for small items.

After that, I went to serve my time to be an agricultural engineer at Hoggarth's, on Sandes Avenue in Kendal. An apprenticeship used to be about five years but that had disappeared out of the system. You never went to college, you just learnt as you went along.

Hoggarth's was kept very busy as the War Ag (War Agricultural Committee) was set up then. Tractors were few and far between on farms as it was mainly horses. The War Ag had tractors and they'd come out and do all the harvesting and ploughing at farms. All this War Ag equipment was kept at Hoggarth's yard and we'd have it to repair. At that time, milking-machines and water-bowls for cow byres were more or less coming in, and we went out installing and repairing them. But there was difficulty in getting parts for farm machinery.

I always remember, Hoggarth's took an old chap on from Troutbeck Bridge just as a handyman for tidying up. Now in the yard we had an old forge and this old lad had been a blacksmith in his early days and managed to get this forge going. Oh, he was a fantastic engineer. Standing in the yard was a binder that was used to cut corn, and one of the teeth in a gear wheel had broken. We couldn't get a new part and the binder wouldn't work. Well, this old lad said, "Can I have a go at that?" He took this wheel off and actually forged a new tooth for it and dove-tailed it back into the binder. A marvellous piece of engineering. He'd get this bloody fire going and you could never see him for smoke in this little shed. But he could do anything, and kept us supplied with spanners he made out of old files.

We more or less covered all of Cumbria from Hoggarth's and had little vans to travel in. Petrol was rationed but, being in agriculture, we had that special allowance for red petrol. A lot of people at that time converted their car engines or tractors to either gas or ran them on TVO, which is like paraffin. You'd start the engine on petrol, keep it really hot and then turn over to the TVO, which smoked like hell.

The farmers weren't responsible for feeding us when we worked on their farms, but it was a known thing that they did feed you. That was one thing about farmers, you got some bloody good meals. And over at West Cumberland when they had pig-killing, they gave the spare-rib part away. So we always got that piece.

Kendal Home Guard (formerly the Borough Band) outside Kendal Parish Hall. Back row, left to right ?, Geoff, Johnie May, Herbert Dinsdale, Bill Troughton (Drum Major), ? Townsend, Jack 'Tic' Wilson, ?,?. Front row, Ernie Gregg, 2nd left, Jack King (Band Master) 4th left, Tony Harrison 3rd right.

Along with two or three other pals, I'd joined the Kendal Borough Band. It was a brass band and a really good one. There'd be about thirty of us in the band, and we had some enjoyable times. I played the tenor horn at first but finished up solo on the flugel horn, which is similar to a cornet but with a deeper tone. We practised at the Abbot Hall, where the art gallery is now.

As the war progressed, the Home Guard came into being and we became the band for them. We swopped our uniform for army uniform, took the Home Guard out on their marches and did training, as well. So we had to go on the rifle range, clean the guns and go to camp. The camp was at this place out near Force Falls at Sedgewick. It was an ammunition dump during the war but was also used as a weekend camp for the Home Guard. We also gave a lot of concerts around Kendal and outlying areas and attended the Service of Remembrance at church every November.

By this time I'd got the urge to join up, so me and a pal volunteered for the Merchant Navy. We had our medicals but my pal was half an inch too small in height and he failed. I passed, but then I had to get permission from my father because I was under twenty-one. Then as I was in a reserved occupation, I had to get permission from my employer to be released. Finally, I needed permission from the Employment Agency. None of them would give their permission, though I pestered and pestered. So I had to give up in the end. Then lo and behold, when I was seventeen and a half, I got bloody called up for the army.

The Motor Transport Section, Durran Hill Carlisle C.1945
Geoff is passenger on the second motor bike from the left

ATS Church Parade at Carlisle.

I had to go up to a place outside Glasgow to do my army training. Well, it was the first time I'd ever been away on my own and to go that distance was a bit scary. When you were called up, you hunted out somebody else that had got their calling up papers, so that you could travel together. There was one lad in Kendal who was going to the same place as me, but the week prior to us going, his father died. As the lad's calling up was postponed, I had to go on my own. I'll always remember getting on the train at Oxenholme and crying my eyes out.

While I was in Scotland, war in Europe was over and there was big celebrations. Lads who lived near the barracks got thirty-six hour passes to go home. The rest of us were on guard duty that night with live ammunition because the Scots went absolutely crazy. At the end of six weeks' training, we did this test of our capabilities. Since I'd worked at Hoggarth's, I wanted to go on the engineering side of R.E.M.E. (Royal Electrical and Mechanical Engineers). I passed all the tests but was posted to the Infantry in the Border Regiment. So along with others, I came down to Durran Hill at Carlisle, the 18th Infantry Training Centre.

Primary training was only your introduction or the basics to the army. But in the infantry, you were actually training for warfare. And we were training for the Japanese War. After six weeks' training, I took ill and had to have another medical. As I was downgraded, this took me out of training. I was put onto the Headquarters staff, and after doing a course at Farnworth as a driver mechanic I came back to Durran Hill as a driving instructor. And it was at

Durran Hill that I met my future wife who was a cook in the A.T.S.

At the end of the eight-week infantry training course, the soldiers did three days on Talking Fell, near Brampton, under actual battle conditions. The infantry had to bivouac out in these awful conditions, and if you were unlucky enough to be sent there, it was hell. As instructors we used to go there with our trucks, which acted as ambulance trucks. Live ammunition was being used, so ten per cent of casualties were allowed for. There were bren guns on tripods with fixed sights and the lads had to go through a battle zone where these guns were firing over their heads.

I remember one incident where they were firing two-inch mortars and one of the lads put a mortar in upside-down. The barrel by this time was red-hot because of the continual firing. The corporal who was in charge saw what had happened and threw himself across this mortar. The mortar exploded and killed him, but he saved these lads. That was the sort of accident which used to happen.

As driving instructors, our main job was to take lads out on six-week courses. We had four training vehicles which were usually fifteen-hundredweight, open-back Bedford's with a canvas cover. There were four trainees to a vehicle. Besides teaching the trainees to drive, they had to be able to do a certain amount of mechanical things as well. We'd take these lads up Wrynose and Hardknott Pass, which were just like cart-tracks in them days. Then we'd ditch the vehicles, roll them off the road, get them bogged down, and the trainees had to get them out again.

On the last week of the course, we'd draw rations out of the stores and bivouac out for three nights. We'd always go to a farm at Sandwich, near Whitehaven, cook for ourselves and have a real good time. Me and the other driving instructor would sleep in the back of the wagon, while the lads slept in the back of the barn.

After VJ (Victory over Japan) Day, I was sent on a course to Aldershot. I didn't expect to be demobbed early on with only joining the army towards the end of the war. But as the war ended, industry started up again and certain specialised people got released from the army. So my boss from Hoggarth's put in for my release, as I came under this category with being an agricultural engineer. I wasn't ten minutes getting my stuff and catching the train back home.

Do you know, I nearly signed back up again. I couldn't settle and was completely lost. I really missed the army way of life even though I hated it when I went in, which most people did. I hated the discipline, though when I was on MT (Motor Transport) we more or less had our freedom. Nobody bothered us because we were called the scourge of the bloody army, with our suits always covered in oil and having these little fiddles going.

One fiddle that I remember was when we were going out for our three-night bivouac. We'd draw rations and petrol for about twenty or thirty men,

Motor Transport Section at Durran Hill, Carlisle. C. 1945
Geoff is on the back row, 3rd left.
Tom Cook from near Penrith is 5th from the right on the back row.

whereas there might only be ten men. All sorts of dodges we'd get up to. At Durran Hill, there was a dance on a Saturday night and they used to allow civvies to come. Our orderly-room clerk asked me if I fancied a Saturday night job helping on the bar and I'd be paid thirty bob. Well, the bar was just a trestle table and the beer was straight from the wood, set up on stillages. Now, all these civilians used to come into the dance late at night and were half slewed. We used to serve them half beer and half water. Oh, we could make a bomb out of it, so we were on a good fiddle.

The pals you have in the army are different from what you have in civvy street. You slept in the same room as your pals, you shared your tales, you went for a drink in the NAFFI together. I really did miss them.

Geoff, now a widower with a family, was a sales/service engineer,
driver and guest-house proprietor before retiring.

FOURTEEN

'You're a policeman now'

∽

Robert Foggin, born Blackhall, County Durham.

I was an apprentice blacksmith at a colliery at Blackhall. When the war started in 1939 I tried to join up, but was told that I was in a reserved occupation and to go back to it. Back at the colliery, I was informed that I'd be sacked if I tried to join up again. I already had two brothers in the navy and two in the army, so I was determined to join up. About three weeks later, I got into the RAF.

In the RAF at last

On August 13 1940 I was stationed at Detling when the Germans raided all the front-line aerodromes in Kent. I've got a book written by the German pilot who was the leader of the raid. He states there was a gruppe (30 aircraft) of JU87 dive-bombers that took off from France and flattened our aerodromes at Middle Wallop and Detling. I think I broke the four-minute mile that day. I remember, during the attack something hit me in the chest and hand. Then my leg got clouted (hit), but I kept running. Everything went black and I finished up in a crater. As I was crawling out, somebody grabbed me and shoved me in the back on a pick-up Bedford and took me to Maidstone City General Hospital. From then on, I was in and out of hospitals being patched up.

After a spell of convalescence at Blackpool, I was sent up here to 5.9 Officers Training Unit at Carlisle. I didn't know what the idea was, being sent up here for a rest, as the 5.9. was being made into a training unit with Hurricanes and that wasn't part of my job. While I was there it was decided, "We can dispense with your services. You're no more use to us."

I didn't go back home, I stayed in digs with a couple at Longtown and was just one of the family. Their name was Tuddenham and they were very nice people and treat me well. While I was at Longtown just kicking my heels, a policeman, old Sergeant Steele, asked, "Do you ever think of joining the police force?" I knew nothing about the police, but he made an application form out, signed it and the Cumberland and Westmorland Police Force sent for me when they were ready.

Because of the freezing of manpower – you maybe won't understand that – there was a Freezing of Manpower Order and police forces weren't allowed to draft in new policemen. They only took what was called War Reserve. So I joined as a War Reserve and was sent to Whitehaven and had digs at 33, The Gardens, Coach Road. My wage was about six pounds, fifteen shillings for a fortnight.

You were given a uniform and gas mask and told, "You're a policeman now," and could go onto the street. It took a bit of getting used to. We carried a little staff (it wasn't called a truncheon in those days), handcuffs, whistle and notebook. I couldn't wear woollen gloves because my false fingers flopped about so I had to wear leather gloves. But the first and biggest job I had to do at Whitehaven was on early morning shift. You had to be sure you went down to the dock with a sandbag and come back with it full of plaice – or you were in trouble.

When you finished your shift, your notebook had to be transcribed word for word into a journal. Even the weather conditions had to be entered daily, so that you could say what the weather was like on such and such a day. Also, anybody of note that you saw had to be wrote down. I don't mean villains, unless they were up to something, of course. But people of note like a vicar. There was one old vicar around at that time and a pompous old ass he was. If you didn't salute him, he reported you to the Inspector.

I was shown around the town by an old fellow, an ex-policeman who'd been called back as a police reservist. We were walking up the Ginns (estate) in Whitehaven on a nice day like this and we got as far as the Canteen Inn. "Come on lad, I'll show you what to do," he said. In we went, and off came his helmet, and it was, "What are you having? Same as me then, a pint?" That's how I learnt to drink pints in uniform. If you did that now, they'd shop you.

On duty you had beats and points. A beat was the area you covered. So at Whitehaven, Ginns was one beat, up at Hensingham was another, and then there was the Town beat. Points were places where you had to be at a certain time, so you could be found if you were needed.

There was also point (traffic) duty. You daren't just stand there, you had to be waving your arms about. I know, because I dropped a clanger when I first did point duty. Inspector Durham, a big fellow, came to see me and I was in the middle of the road at Duke Street and there was nothing doing. So I took a fag out and lit it. Inspector Durham said, "What do you think you're doing? Put it out, or you'll get me hung." I'd forgotten where I was.

It was rare that anybody hit a policeman. Any bad lads you caught, there was no hassle. There was quite a few Norwegians around. Hard drinkers they were, but not a lot of trouble, expect a little one who was only about the

size of my missus. They weren't a bad lot. It was just a bit of high jinks and the life that they were leading. Same with the miners, they were good-hearted.

The biggest trouble was me. At that time I hadn't been to Stanley

Grange, the police training college at Preston. So I'd be walking along up the street with the Inspector, Edward Nixon, and he'd say, "Do you know your law and can you define larceny?" Well, as far as I knew, it was when somebody nicked something.

Then we'd walk on and come to these old dears queuing for fags or whatever. I'd be told they mustn't obstruct the footpath. So I had the rotten job of telling these old lasses with their shawls wrapped round them, "Come on now ladies, you'll have to stand off the footpath." Then there was muttering and shouting, "My lad's away fighting for you, you young bugger. You should be in the bloody army." What could I tell them? I had nothing to prove I'd been in the forces, so I had to take what they gave me.

It was a while before I knew that I was entitled to wear a 'wound stripe' on my uniform. That's what I had to say, I'd been in the war. You see, there was a stigma attached to reservists because a lot of them were bloody skivers who didn't want to fight, and I didn't want to be one of them. I took some stick, I can tell you.

At Whitehaven there was a lot of warehouses on the dock-side and they had firewatchers in them every night. I was on duty with another bobby one night and a firewatcher invited us in for a cup of coffee. Well, the bobby was stringing this poor beggar along that a chap had committed suicide in this warehouse. You know what these old warehouses are like, with bits of rope hanging down from the beams. Folk working there cut the rope down instead of unhooking it. This bobby was saying, "Aye, it happened right here. I'll never forget that." The firewatcher wouldn't stop in the building after that. He was so scared, he just stood in the doorway every night.

Then there was one New Year's Eve when an old sergeant said, "I'm sorry, but you're stuck up on the Ginns beat." I thought, "That's champion." Anyway, he said he'd meet me near the Canteen Inn half-way through my shift to sign my pocket book. Later that night when he met me, this sergeant said, "There's a right carry-on going on in there. Do you know what's going on?" "Yes", I said, "I've just come out of there." "Right, replied the sergeant, "We'll go back in." Well, he got as tight as a tick and was even drinking out of a cut-glass vase. I had to take him home, get his house keys out of his pocket, open the door and leave him in the hall passage. Next night on duty he said, "Give me a wide berth. I got a real doggin' off my missus because of you."

After all that I was sent to Stanley Grange, the police training college at Preston, to learn to be a policeman. That was grand. Captain Horden was the Chief Constable there, and had been in the Flying Corps in the First World War. There was five of us sent from Cumberland for this course. We were all on parade in uniform when the Sergeant said, "Right, everyone's dismissed except you. The Chief wants to see you in his office. I didn't know what to expect but I was in there about an hour, talking about aeroplanes. He was a real nice fellow. I enjoyed my time there.

Back from Stanley Grange I was sent to Maryport and had digs with Mrs Temple at No 1, Ellenborough Place. My beat was the town and I was tied to the docks. A lot of boats used the harbour. Instead of taking them to the big ports where boats were getting bombed, they'd be brought up to Maryport and Silloth for safety. Also, we used to get coal boats coming in from the Irish Free State. We had to check the sailors as there used to be a lot of them who brought butter in from Ireland, so there was a bit of black-marketing going on. But on the docks at that time you could buy a good-sized skate for half-a-crown, and a bucket of small fish for sixpence.

There was quite a bit of activity going on up at Silloth and Kirkbride with the aerodromes. They called the Solway Firth 'Hudson Bay' because they were flying Hudson's over that area. The pilots were just training, and if they were disorientated they would land on what they thought was sand, but it was quick sands. I know the pilots used to shoot at big targets in the Solway when they were doing shooting exercises. These targets were big wooden structures with huge cork boxing so they wouldn't sink if they were punctured.

After Maryport I was sent up to Penrith where there was more going on. There was a lot of soldiers down at Lowther and they had a special light, like a laser, that they were trying to perfect for tanks. Every now and again the sky would light up when this light was being tested.

Penrith was used as a staging depot for refurbished army wagons going south. These were driven by little dead-beats from Glasgow who created mayhem in the pubs round here. The Saturday night dances in the drill hall used to be a free-for-all.

There was only two policewomen in the force at the back-end of the war. Before they came, it was policemen's wives who

WARTIME PRECAUTIONS IN PENRITH.

Policemen's Steel Helmets : Sandbagged Buildings.

Penrith, in common with other towns, though far from the scenes of conflict, shows many signs of precaution against the air arm of modern warfare.

Kerbs, walls, railings and lamp posts are chequered with white paint to give some degree of visibility on these nights of enshrouding darkness.

The police carry with them steel helmets and—as everyone else is advised to do—their gas masks, while also patrolling the streets are special constables distinguished by their armlets.

Public buildings—the Town Hall, Drill Hall, Police Station, St. Andrew's Parish Rooms (a first aid post), Labour Exchange, Cottage Hospital, Isolation Hospital, and Gas Works—are all protected with formidable barricades of sandbags, in the filling of which members of the British Legion gave valuable assistance. Lorries brought the sand from Cowrake Quarry.

Then at nights there is not—or should not be—a light to be seen, and while the black-out may not be 100 per cent. complete the glimmers in the gloom are very few and far between, thanks to the effective measures taken by householders to screen their windows.

The severe lighting restrictions on motor vehicles virtually impose a speed limit, so bad is visibility, and one sympathises particularly with the drivers of long distance transports, whose task must be exceedingly difficult.

And all the while, in daytime or darkness, there are listening ears at the Town Hall—the nerve centre of the A.R.P. organisation over a wide area—which is continuously manned.

Mr. John Jackson, Divisional Controller of the Penrith Report Centre, wishes to thank all those ladies and gentlemen who so willingly responded to the appeal for helpers; the British Legion for their willing help given in dealing with sandbags; the Newcastle Royal Grammar School boys who helped in the filling of sandbags, and the Headmaster for kindly giving permission to employ them; and all the staff of the Report Centre for their arduous and loyal work.

used to deal with any female prisoners we had. You see, it was all different in those days. You couldn't be posted to your own home town and you even had to ask permission to get married. Then, if your wife was working, they frowned on that.

At the end of the war the freezing of manpower was rescinded and recruits were taken on. Quite a lot of them were ex-servicemen. Mr Baron, the Deputy Chief Constable, sent for me and asked if I wanted to be 'a regular' or apply to join the police. Now, the difference was that as a war reservist I could stay on and be absorbed into the police force. Or I could officially apply to join the police, sit an entrance examination and, if I passed, I could be taken on.

To me, the fact I was just a war reservist and been kept on in the police would look as though I'd got in through the back door. So I chose to sit the entrance exam, as I thought I'd rather join. Anyway I passed the exam and went away to Bruche, which is the Police Training College at Warrington. This was the first intake and we were in wooden huts, which had been the Yankee air force accommodation. So that's how I started my career in the police force.

Married with a family, Bob served for thirty two years in the police force and is now a chiropodist.

(Bob died shortly before this book was completed. I am indebted to his family for giving their permission to include his story).

FIFTEEN

'What about starting a band?'

Dennis Moorhouse, *born 1923 at Natland.*

I went to Kendal Grammar School and left in 1938 to start work on the family farm. Well, the way things were looking then, I'd say we did expect war. You know, with Germany getting a lot of power and one thing and another.

Just after the war started in '39 we got two evacuees on the farm. They stayed a month or two, and then moved on. Then when the bombing started at Barrow, we got an evacuee from there. I don't think any of them settled in too well at the start. The problem was, they weren't clothed properly. They were poor people and hadn't the clothes. I gave one of these evacuees a pair of my shoes. The shoes that he came in had nails sticking through the bottom. The lad couldn't walk. It was terrible. They seemed to be better dressed as the war went on but at the start, oh dearie me. I felt sorry for them.

The war made a lot of difference on the farm. It brought a lot more work. You see, farmers were allocated a lot of ploughing to do. Half the country was back-side up (dug up and ploughed), for growing stuff. We used to grow corn and turnips because you couldn't buy feed for cattle. You had to produce so much milk before you were allowed coupons for feed. And in those days people didn't produce a lot of milk on the farms round here.

MILK PRICES FIXED FOR 18 MONTHS

BELOW is the schedule of prices which will be paid to producers up to 31st March, 1945. These prices absorb the balance of the increase of 1d. per gallon awarded to milk producers by the Government, as from 1st October, 1943, after allocating (as already announced) 0.7d. per gallon of the award to enable the revised transport rates to be introduced on 1st December, 1943.

In addition to these prices the Board will pay the War Time Production Bonus, as follows :—

(*a*) January to March, 1944, and October, 1944, to March, 1945, at 1½d. per gallon on the first 400 gallons for each producer.

(*b*) April to September, 1944, at ½d. per gallon on the first 500 gallons for each producer.

PRODUCERS' PRICES: OCTOBER, 1943—MARCH, 1945
(PER GALLON)

	1 Northern	2 North Western	3 Eastern	4 East Midland	5 West Midland	6 North Wales	7 South Wales	8 Southern	9 Mid-Western	10 Far-Western	11 South Eastern	*Increase over corresponding month of 1942-3
	s. d.	s. d.	s. d.	s. d.	s. d.	s. d.	s. d.	s. d.	s. d.	s. d.	s. d.	d.
October, 1943	2 2	2 2	2 2	2 2¼	2 1¾	2 1¾	2 1¾	2 2¼	2 1¾	2 1¾	2 2¼	—
November ..	2 6¼	2 6¼	2 6¼	2 6¼	2 6	2 6	2 6	2 6¼	2 5¾	2 5¾	2 6¼	—
December ..	2 8½	2 8¾	2 8¾	2 8¾	2 8¾	2 8¾	2 8½	2 9	2 8¾	2 8½	2 9	1¼
January, 1944	2 7½	2 7½	2 7¾	2 7¾	2 7½	2 7½	2 7¾	2 7¾	2 7½	2 7½	2 8	¼
February ..	2 6¼	2 6¼	2 6½	2 6½	2 6¼	2 6¼	2 6½	2 6½	2 6¼	2 6¼	2 6¾	¼
*March	2 3¼	2 3¼	2 3½	2 3¼	2 3¼	2 3¼	2 3½	2 3½	2 3¼	2 3¼	2 3¾	¼
April	1 8¾	1 8¾	1 9	1 8¾	1 8½	1 8½	1 8¾	1 9	1 8¾	1 8½	1 9	1½
May	1 3¾	1 3¾	1 3¾	1 4	1 3¾	1 3¾	1 3¾	1 4	1 3¾	1 3¾	1 4¼	¼
June	1 3¾	1 3¾	1 4	1 3¾	1 3¾	1 3¾	1 3¾	1 4	1 3¾	1 3½	1 4	¼
July	1 5½	1 5½	1 5½	1 5½	1 5¼	1 5½	1 5½	1 5¾	1 5¼	1 5¼	1 5¾	¼
August	1 6¾	1 6¾	1 7	1 6¾	1 6½	1 6¾	1 6¾	1 6¾	1 6½	1 6½	1 7	¼
September ..	1 7	1 7	1 7	1 7	1 7	1 7	1 7	1 7¼	1 7	1 6¾	1 7¼	¼
October ..	2 2¼	2 2¼	2 2¼	2 2½	2 2	2 2	2 2	2 2½	2 2	2 2	2 2½	¼
November ..	2 6¾	2 6¾	2 6¾	2 6¾	2 6½	2 6½	2 6½	2 6¾	2 6¼	2 6¼	2 6¾	½
December ..	2 7¾	2 8	2 8	2 8	2 8	2 8	2 7¾	2 8¼	2 8	2 7¾	2 8¼	½
January, 1945	2 7½	2 7½	2 7¾	2 7¾	2 7½	2 7½	2 7¾	2 7¾	2 7½	2 7½	2 8	¼
February ..	2 6¼	2 6¼	2 6½	2 6½	2 6¼	2 6¼	2 6½	2 6½	2 6¼	2 6¼	2 6¾	¼
*March	2 3¼	2 3¼	2 3½	2 3¼	2 3¼	2 3¼	2 3½	2 3½	2 3¼	2 3¼	2 3¾	¼

*Provisional

WAR-TIME PRODUCTION BONUS

In addition to the above prices, producers will receive—

(*a*) 1½d. per gallon on the first 400 gallons sold by wholesale and retail in each of the nine months January–March, 1944, and October, 1944–March, 1945.

and (*b*) ½d. per gallon on the first 500 gallons sold by wholesale and retail in each of the six months April–September, 1944.

12 THE HOME FARMER

We used horses then and it was hard work. You were working all hours of the day and just had to get on with it. Like, all the corn was to thresh, there was no combine harvesters. We'd usually a fortnight's threshing in September or October. Then there was pulling all the turnips and getting all the potatoes out. It was one thing after another. You were never done.

The price of livestock was regulated. At Kendal Auction Mart the top price for calves was about two guineas. Then the price went down to about thirty bob, and there was a lower price than that. But it was the times, you see. There wasn't the haulage into the auction marts, no cattle wagons, and people used to walk their stock to market.

There was still the hirings during the war years when people used to get hired at Whitsun or Martimas. But of course, there wasn't the same amount of labour. Also, you were only allowed to have labour according to the size of your farm. Like, a smallish farm would only be allowed one or two labourers and a big farmer would maybe have three.

You could get prisoners to help out from Bela Camp down at Milnthorpe. You used to pay the Government for them to help out with threshing and such like. They were all right, were these prisoners. If you gave them plenty of packets of cigarettes, they'd work like troopers. I know at one threshing day we had fourteen of these prisoners and there was only one that could speak English. He had to tell the others what to do.

They were Italian lads that we used to get, and my mother made them their dinners and teas. Then at half-past five at night, the wagon would pick them up to take them back to Bela Camp. One or two of these prisoners came to live on nearby farms to help out. I think they were glad to get out of the war, really.

Farmers were allowed to keep two pigs per year for themselves so there was the black market. There was a man used to come round here and it was, "Have you any hams?" and you got quite a decent price for a ham. The local bobbies didn't bother. Like, the local policeman would get half-a-dozen eggs and a bit of bacon for himself, so he'd turn a blind eye.

You could also keep any amount of hens. You see, with growing corn you fed them on that. Also, these hens were all outside, there was no intensive (battery breeding) and they used to be scratching about. So even though food was scarce, I think farmers were about as well off as anybody.

Yes, I was in Dad's Army. You had to be about sixteen or seventeen to join the Home Guard, so I'd join in about 1941. And with me working on the farm, I was in a deferred occupation. I got all the papers to join up but they were scrapped because I was on the farm, you see.

On a Sunday morning, all of us in the Home Guard went to St Mark's Home, down in the village, because that's where the playing field was and

HOME GUARD

INSTRUCTION No. 19—1940

SENTRIES

(This instruction supersedes Appendix B to L.D.V. Instruction 5.)

1. Sentries guarding vulnerable points
   i. The following instructions will be observed by sentries guarding vulnerable points :—
   (a) Any person approaching a post will be challenged—
   " HALT ! WHO GOES THERE ? "
   The sentry must be perfectly certain that his challenge is given in the loudest possible manner, so that even those who may be dull of hearing can have the chance of responding—
   " FRIEND "
   (or giving some similar indication regarding his identity).
   (b) A person having responded to the challenge in this way is expected to remain halted. The sentry will then call out—
   " ADVANCE ONE—TO BE RECOGNIZED ".
   By " one," one person is meant. If the party challenged comprises more than one person, the sentry will repeat this order for each member of the party and only one will advance in response to the order. If the credentials of the person who approaches the post are in order, he will be allowed to pass, but if not he will be detained and the guard turned out.
   (c) If a person who is challenged under (a) does not halt, he will then be challenged again by the sentry—
   " HALT, OR I FIRE ".
   (d) If a person does not halt after this warning, he will be challenged once again in the same manner. If he does not halt, and if no means are available to stop him, it is then the duty of the sentry to use his rifle and shoot—aiming low to hit but not to kill. The sentry must remember that it is his duty to stop a person from advancing further should he fail to respond to the challenge and warning.
   (e) If a person can be stopped in any other way, for example, by calling to the guard to assist, then the sentry will not shoot. The sentry must use his intelligence and sense of responsibility to decide whether he will shoot or not.
   (f) At night or in thick fog, a sentry must not allow himself to be rushed and he must be well on the alert, more so than in daylight. He must be ready to take such action as is necessary to prevent any person who refuses to respond to his challenge and warning from approaching closer to his sentry post.
   ii. Os.C. units or stations who are responsible for issuing orders to sentries guarding vulnerable points will take immediate action to comply with these instructions.
   iii. The above forms of challenge by sentries supersede those laid down in the Manual of Elementary Drill (All Arms) where they are at variance with the above.

2. Control of road traffic
   The action to be taken at posts where it is desired to restrict the free movement of traffic will vary with the locality concerned, but will be generally on the following lines :—
   i. By day, sentries will halt traffic by ordinary police signals ; by night, a red lamp will be waved.

we could exercise. Wednesday nights we went down to the old Natland School for lectures and one thing and another. It would be about six months after I joined the Home Guard that we got guns. Once we had them, we used to go onto the rifle range at Kendal and Kirkby Lonsdale for gun practise. That was quite interesting.

There's a place not far from here, on the road to Sedgewick, called Larkrigg Hill. That's where we used to go when they thought there was going to be an invasion. It was parachutists we were supposed to be after. This hill had good views and you could see for miles around. It was a rota job. We went to Larkrigg Hill on a rota about once a week. Say, about from four till seven o'clock in the morning and again at night.

It was in 1944 that this friend of mine, Jack Bennett, who could play the drums, said, "What about starting a band?" There was a good musician called Mary Allan and she seemed keen on the idea. Next we got a young fella from Kendal who could play the accordion. I could also play the accordion and piano, so we started up and called ourselves 'The Mayfair.'

By that time of the war people were having these 'do's' for Welcome Home Funds and one thing and another. And you see, all the village halls were used for dances and socials. Stainton's, the coach people in Kendal, also had taxis which we hired to take us around.

We played at Burneside, Dent, Newbiggin-on-Lune, Arnside, Storth, Levens, Carnforth and Silverdale. In fact we played from up near Carlisle to Carnforth in the south. As for pay, the musicians' union rates were six shillings and eight-pence an hour. The music we played was what was

The Mayfair Band
Left to right, Jeff Dodds, Dennis Moorehouse,
Colin Dixon &Mary Allen

available on sheet music but it was the popular stuff, music of the day. We didn't have a vocalist – we didn't get that far. You see, there was no back-up with electrical equipment. Very few places had microphones, it was all new at that time.

We wore dress-suits, and I was lucky as I had two. The mother of a local lad who'd been killed at Arnham wanted me to have his suit. She didn't want paying, just wanted coupons for it. So I gave her the coupons and got a good suit. I think my wife only done away with it about two years since, so it lasted well.

Sometimes only three of us could play on certain nights. Other times, all four of us, and maybe even five when a trumpet and trombone player came with us. At that time there was only two other bands in Kendal, The Arcadians and The Blue Rascals. If we couldn't make an engagement, one of the other bands would stand in for us and we'd do the same for them.

The socials we played at, nearly all had a whist drive and then a dance after that. The price for folk going to these do's was from one shilling and sixpence, up to half-a-crown. Mostly it was winter when we played as there was too much work to do in summer. Especially among the farmers, they hadn't the time to go. So our bookings were usually from the end of

September, right through till lambing time in Spring.

Mind you, it could be difficult travelling in winter. I know one night we went to Great Asby and it was a wild night. The river was overflowing in the village and all the lights were down when we got there. We wondered where everybody was, so we went to the local pub and that's where they all were. We got some temporary lighting fit up and we played until half-past two in the morning.

There was many a time it was four o'clock in the morning when I was coming home with the band, and I started work at half-past six. As I was only in my early twenties in those years, it didn't matter. Finally one of the chaps left the band and work got the better of me. You see, my father had arthritis and I had to stop at home and do extra work. So The Mayfair disbanded but it had been quite an interesting time.

Dennis, a married man with a family is now a retired farmer.

SIXTEEN

'My car was parked up in the barn'

∽

Dorothy Ridley, born 1916 at Grimsby but living at Hastings at the outbreak of the war.

Yes, definitely I knew there was going to be a war. Everybody down Hastings was sure there was going to be a war. I can remember, after Munich I was helping to deliver out gas masks at St Leonard's and we worked really hard. I drove my car, delivering gas masks chiefly to housebound elderly people. That was before war was declared.

Then when war was declared in 1939, from September until about the following April, there was nothing much happening at all. When war started in earnest, you could hear and see the guns firing from the French coast. On the South coast, sirens used to go off every single night as the German planes started to come over. When the troops came back from Dunkirk, some landed at Hastings pier and some of them had hardly any clothes.

I was running a very small hotel at the time. My mother, who was a widow, had bought the hotel, letting the bedrooms mostly to families with young children as we both loved children. Unfortunately she died, and when the war came, I didn't get a lot of holiday-makers. So I eventually sold the hotel. Almost gave it away, really, as no-one was coming to Hastings for holidays, with it being so near the French coast.

By that time I knew I'd have to do something for the war effort, but I didn't know what. Then a lady advertised in the weekly paper to say she was going to interview people interested in doing forestry work in the Land Army. So I went to see her, decided I liked the sound of forestry work, and went to the Forest of Dean to do my training.

I was at the Forest of Dean for about six weeks and was provided with the Land Army clothes. There was knee-breeches, long socks, dungarees, thick green jerseys, airtex shirts, wellington boots, a big overcoat and a felt hat. We were trained to do various things, such as how to measure standing and falling timber and to work out the cubic capacity of trees. Then we were given a list of places where we could apply to work and a lot of them were up north.

Myself and another girl were sent up to Appleby and we stayed at a private house with a Mr and Mrs Alderson. My car, a little red Austin 7 sports car, came up later on by railway to Appleby. I suppose it was unusual for a woman to have a sports car in those days. And I never passed a driving test, as I had a licence before tests were compulsory. I think the licence would automatically allow me to drive motorbikes and tractors. However, I couldn't use the car very often because of the petrol rationing, so I never used it for work.

Our work was measuring timber at Hoff Lunn, a very big wood between Appleby and Orton. At first the two of us biked to work but one of the men who was felling trees had a van, so we used to crowd in with other men who were also going up to the woods.

I stayed at Appleby for three months and moved to Cliburn, as by that time I was working at Whinfell. My car was parked up in a barn at Cliburn while first of all I stayed at the village pub. Then I moved into a private house with two elderly ladies. They were farmers' daughters, called Mary and Ethel, and were very nice, very kind. I didn't pay much for my digs, maybe about thirty shillings.

My wage was about three pounds and that was a fairly good wage for women. The men that I worked with were mostly local and married. A lot of them had been farm workers, but forestry work was better paid. One man with a wife and two children had worked as a roadman for the council. His wage had only been thirty-eight shillings a week.

I enjoyed my work, but, with coming from the South, I found the weather very cold in winter, and there were a few days when we couldn't get to work because of the snow. It was about a mile and a half to walk from Cliburn up to the woods. Sometimes wagons would pick us up on the way to work and give us a lift. One summer we moved right down by the River Eden where they were felling trees. That was beautiful because it was a lovely summer and we could go swimming when we weren't very busy.

My job had changed from what I expected it to be. I thought I was going to be outside measuring timber. But eventually every day I worked half a day measuring up in the saw-mill. The other half was spent doing the books in the office. I had preferred working outside because it was very noisy in the saw-mill. But I enjoyed the work, whatever I was doing.

A lot of the wood went to be used as pit props or railway sleepers, and some was used as ordinary planks. There was quite a lot of village girls who used to work on the land with us. They used to saw some of the pit props, or maybe be stacking wood. It was surprising how well the girls got on together, being from different towns and the country. But during the war everybody did get on well together. The men were mostly in their late thirties, and we also had one or two conscientious objectors, who were such nice lads.

'Dorothy having a breather'

I think we worked from half-past eight in the morning until four or five in the afternoon. You see, you had to work while it was daylight. At nights we'd bike to dances at the various villages round about. It wasn't very dear then to go to a dance, about one shilling or one shilling and sixpence. There wasn't an awful lot of troops around to go to these dances. I think a few came from a little air-field fairly nearby and it was too far away for the ones at Warcop.

On a Saturday we worked until midday and then walked over to the Appleby road and caught a bus to Penrith that came from Darlington. We went to Penrith every Saturday, did some shopping, and then we'd go to the first house pictures. When the film finished we used to rush out to the railway station. If you missed the train you had to walk back to Cliburn and that was about six or seven miles. There was no buses running at that time of night. I missed

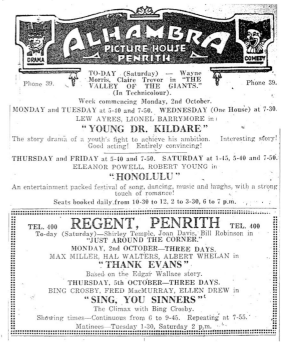

the trains a couple of times but really, it didn't bother me. I was courting my future husband at the time, who also lived at Cliburn. So, with another couple, we'd set off and walk back to the village.

We had a local bobby in Cliburn, Tommy Hood, and he would have quite a big area to cover, which included Morland and Crossrigg. There was also evacuees in the village, and my landladies had a little boy called Tommy who I think was from Barrow-in-Furness.

I suppose there was a bit of a black market in the country, but you see, in the villages everyone had gardens and you could always get potatoes and carrots. My landladies' brother was a farmer so I can't remember going short of any food.

The girl that originally came with me from the Forest of Dean only stayed about a month as she didn't like it. Then another girl came who was from Birkenhead way, and she stayed for quite a long time until she left and joined the WRENS. Just before I left Cliburn, a youth hostel was built for land girls who were working on the farms. It's the village hall now.

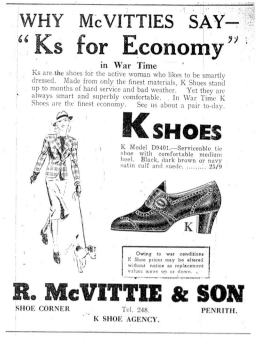
As I had no relations at Hastings, I used to visit an aunt in Grimsby twice a year when I was on leave. So that was always a problem, as Grimsby was a bad (awkward) place to get to. You had to travel by train to Settle, change there for Leeds, then again at Doncaster. Grimsby did get quite a lot of bombing but I was lucky, as there was never much when I was there. My aunt was elderly, and as she didn't need her clothing coupons, she gave them to me.

I'd met my future husband, Jack at Cliburn, where he lived. He was a driver for Shap Granite Works and drove all over the place. Maybe over to Billingham, up to Ayr or down to Liverpool or Manchester. I know he drove an Albian lorry for a while and then a big E.R.F. The granite works were making big pipes, flag-stones and gravel. That was why he went to bring cement back from Billingham.

We got married in 1943 at Cliburn village church. I wore a pale blue suit for my wedding and had to use coupons to buy it, which was a bother. In those days children used to tie the church gates so that you had to throw them money to untie them. One of the tractors from work was across the road, and we had to throw more pennies for that to be moved.

Our wedding reception was at my sister-in-law's house in the village, and we had a wedding cake made by one of the villagers. Somebody had managed to get fruit for the cake, so we did rather well. Mary and Ethel, my landladies, were very kind, as until we got a house, we lived with them.

It was about six months later when we moved to our house at Shap. The first one we were offered by the Shap Granite Company had only a cold water tap and an outside toilet. Fortunately another one became vacant, which was in a better condition, and we moved into that.

There was an awful lot of traffic and troop movement going over Shap night and day, as that was the main road up to Scotland. It was similar to what a motorway is today. We had the road in front of our house and the main railway line behind. But after a while you didn't notice the noise. When the weather was bad over Shap, quite a number of the houses took transport drivers overnight, or sometimes longer. If the drivers couldn't get accommodation they used to sleep in the village hall.

After we moved to Shap my grandmother came to live with us. As she was very old I managed to get some petrol coupons to take her out in the car. Just imagine, an old lady of ninety years of age going out in a sports car! It wasn't many coupons we had, but we managed to go and see Jack's sister. She lived on a farm at Lazonby, and we could get some butter and eggs.

I stopped work in 1944 and my daughter was born later that year. Oh, heck no, there wasn't the facilities there is today. I knew about this little nursing home at Penrith and went there. It wasn't very expensive, about ten pounds, and I had a room to myself. In those days you weren't allowed to get out of bed and walk around, you know. It wasn't this twenty-four-hour business and you were allowed home. You were meant to stay in bed for a fortnight, but I only stayed ten days as I wanting to get home.

The funny thing was, when I was living down at Hastings, expectant mothers were sent down there from London. Well, it was crazy, wasn't it? It was one of the nearest places to the French coast. I suppose they never thought the Germans would get as far as Hastings.

When the war finished in 1945 we had a party for the children at Shap. Mothers made all the food and it was put on long trestles in our back gardens. Afterwards, the children played games. However, the end of the war didn't mean the end of stranded drivers at Shap.

When my children were old enough I went to work in the school canteen, which was in the village hall. Very often in bad weather, we went into the hall in the morning, where the drivers were staying. As you can imagine, there was a lot of clearing away before we could start work. If the weather was very bad, often the electricity went off. Than meant we had to make fires in the school-rooms and cook the children's meals over the fires. Looking back, we had some quite exciting times in that village hall.

Dorothy is now a widow with a family.

SEVENTEEN

'Can I have a pair of kippers?'

∽

Leonard Palmer, *born 1921 at Seaton, near Workington*

I joined the Territorial Army in 1937. There'd been a big recruitment drive and you were told that if you joined the TA you could pick your own regiment. However, if you didn't join and a war was ever declared, you could be shoved anywhere. So I joined the TA and was in the Workington 51 Field Regiment. That was the Artillery for the 203 and 204 Battery and our Headquarters were at Edkin Street in Workington. Others that joined were John Mason, a chap called Freddie Kershe, whose family had a furniture shop down on Hagg Hill, and Stan Williams, who worked in the electrical department of the Co-op at Oxford Street. Our Colonel was Duncan Patterson, who lived on Calva Brow in a big red house.

I was working at our fresh fish shop in Washington Street at that time, along with my father, Uncle Alan and Uncle Herbert. We got our fresh fish from Aberdeen, Hull, Grimsby and Fleetwood. Kippers came from Seahouses and Buckie, and skate was from Workington Docks. We also stocked rabbits that we bought from local farmers and Dad bought poultry for the shop at Cockermouth market every Monday.

Palmer's Shop 1931

Most people ate a lot more fish than they do today. You see, both before the war and during it, there was about forty fish-and-chip shops in Workington. Most of them were run from people's front parlours, as there wasn't the rules and regulations then about running businesses.

Round here, fish was mostly fried. Fried cod or haddock in batter. Though finnan haddock, that's the yellow fish, they used to steam it. My dad used to sell coarse sprats. This was cod, filleted and salted – salt fish. Years back, when the old wooden boats used to come into Workington, that was the sailors' diet. It was an Irishman's meal – potatoes and salt fish. To cook it, you'd cut up a piece of salt fish, put it in water overnight, then boil it and eat it with potatoes. Grocers used to sell salt fish. They used to have it on display outside their shops and dogs used to widdle on it as they went past. That's true.

In them days, people queued for fish every day the shop was due to open. We closed on a Monday, but when fish was delivered on a Tuesday, we could be sold out by dinner time. I had an old three-wheeler van and used to deliver fish from that. I'd deliver fish to the Victoria Hotel and Fish Hotel at Buttermere, then go on to Thackthwaite, that's just outside Lorton, one day a week. On other days I'd deliver to Camerton, Siddick, Clifton and Seaton. So you'd go around a lot of little villages and farmhouses and be invited in for a cup of tea before setting off back home.

In the summer of 1939, the 203 and 204 Battalions went to the firing camp in Wales for a fortnight. We were mostly lads from Cumbria. Lads from Whitehaven, Aspatria, Maryport and Workington. We took our guns, 45 howitzers and something like a boffa gun, quick-firing anti-aircraft guns with us, which we used on the big range at Wales. The wagon I had was called a wireless buggy, and Bobby Buchanan from Workington, he used to roll the wire from the back of the buggy to fix to the telephone wires. That's what we also practised at this camp. I remember our meals could be a tin of corned beef and a slice of bread. Real army stuff. Oh gee, it was terrible. But there you are, that's army life. The weather at the camp was red-hot and we came back as brown as berries.

One Friday in September 1939, I was on the van delivering fish to the Victoria Hotel at Buttermere. When I came back at teatime my dad said there'd been a message for me to report back to the Drill Hall. With everybody else, I reported back to the Drill Hall but we were told we had to go back the next day. The next day, the same thing happened. We were told to go back on the Sunday.

The following day was Sunday 3 September 1939. Along with all the other territorials I went to the Drill Hall, and this time we were marched up to Workington Hall. There was about five hundred of us and Colonel

Patterson said, "Now lads, I've got some news for you. War's been declared." We all gave a good cheer before marching back to the Drill Hall. That's when we got our shilling, The King's shilling for joining the army. Then you could have a pint to drink, even those who were only seventeen. I didn't, because I daren't go home smelling of drink with my dad being there. That Sunday had been a lovely sunny morning but within half-an-hour of war being declared, the heavens opened. The rain came down like stair-rods and town was nearly flooded. I remember somebody said, "Aye well, that's an act of God." You know, good and bad in such a short space of time, just like war.

The following morning we all lined up and were put onto these buses and taken to Carlisle. At Carlisle we stayed at the old Market Hall, that's the cattle market down Botchergate and had our meals in the Gretna Tavern. We didn't do much at first, in fact we went and picked potatoes for the farmers. We got nothing for doing it, not even a cup of tea. Then the lads amongst us who were nineteen years old from the battery, were picked out to go to Norway. The rest of us who were too young to go, went to Liverpool and joined the anti-aircraft units. Then as driving instructors at Liverpool,

Len at Milan, October 1945

Blackpool and Hull. After that I was transferred to Doncaster, and that's where I met the wife. Then I was sent abroad until after the end of the war.

Before going abroad, I used to come home on leave. The war made a big difference to the fish shop. People didn't need coupons for fish but the trade was controlled by the Ministry of Agriculture. Our local branch was in Washington Street at Workington, just below the New Crown pub. The price of fish was controlled by the Ministry and they controlled your quota. A pound of cod or haddock was about one shilling and eight pence, or up to two shillings. Kippers were usually four-pence a pair. But we didn't know what fish was being sent to us. There could be cod, haddock or small plaice. It came in a box, maybe a box of plaice and that was it. You just had to sell what was sent, there was no choice. The fish was rationed to the shops. Maybe before the war you needed five stone of fish. Well, during the war it was cut right down to maybe two stone that you were sent. But there was still some fishing done out of Workington, mostly skate and cod.

Even though coupons weren't needed for fish, there wasn't the supply for the demand. So you always got some people who'd come into the shop and say, "Can I have a pair of kippers and a pair of whatever else there is?" My dad and uncle Alan tried to be quite fair with everybody and would say, "Oh no, sorry. You're only allowed so much." You see, these folks would say they were shopping for somebody else as well as themselves, but they weren't.

Fat that was needed to cook the fish was also allocated and the amount was cut down from pre-war days. But it was nice fat that we got. We enjoyed it and at the time didn't know where it came from.. It wasn't until years later when I took some salmon down to Blackpool and got talking to somebody in the trade that I found out. They told me the name of the place where the fat came from in West Cumberland during the war. I said, "Good gracious, that's the knackers' yard."

It was difficult getting rabbits and poultry during the war. Just after the war started, the local brewery put a big order in for poultry at Christmas time. My dad went to the usual farmers he bought off when he needed extra poultry and they turned round and said, "Oh, we're selling what we have to our regular milk customers." Same with rabbits. Whereas my dad would give a farmer ten-pence to a shilling for a rabbit, farmers could sell them for up to two shillings at a time to their milk customers.

However, with petrol being in short supply, the three-wheeler van was taken off the road, so no-one went round the outlying areas. But with the shortage of fish, there wouldn't have been much if anything to sell.

When I came home, I would just be on seven days leave. What was noticeable was the amount of soldiers in the town, they were all over the place. They were in the Town Hall, Drill Hall, Princess Hall, Hippodrome Dance Hall, and at Workington Hall which was in full swing then. What I couldn't weigh up was, they used to send the Workington lads (soldiers) down to London and the London lads up to Workington.

When the war finished, I was in Salonika and wasn't demobbed until 1946. Trade for fish was thriving after the war. When I took over the shop on my own, I brought the wife in to help me and we were doing all right. We supplied fish for school meals from as far as Dalston in the north, down to Millom in the south of the county. Fish was in good demand until the scare about radioactivity in the Irish Sea. That's what killed trade round here.

Retirement Day for Mr and Mrs Palmer

Len, now a widow with a family was a fishmonger until retirement.

EIGHTEEN

'There were very few young men left'

cᴏɑ

Bill Jackson, born 1928 at Allithwaite.

I can remember the Sunday that war was declared very well. The radio broadcast was on and my mother broke down and cried. Her youngest brother was in the Territorials and she knew he'd be right on the front line. Yes, I can remember that day vividly.

The war made a big difference round here because of recruiting. Within a few years there was very few young men left in the eighteen to forty age bracket. They recruited them all. There was just the old ones or essential workers left. So it was all hands to the pump. Anybody that had any land, grew their own vegetables to be self-supporting. There was this slogan, 'Dig for Victory', but people didn't need much encouragement. They grew as much as possible because they were so limited in the food they could get. They grew something on every available inch in their gardens.

At the beginning of the war, the airfield and army camp for the Royal Artillery were built next to each other at Cark-in-Cartmel. We farmed land adjoining there and had a good view of what was happening. The air force were taught to fly in Hansons, very old planes they were, and used to pull silk targets across the sky for the artillery to shoot at. If these silk targets came down, oh, everybody was running to get a piece because it was pure silk and ladies used it to make their underwear.

It was said when Allithwaite was bombed that somebody on the army camp was trigger happy, let go with their guns and gave us away. You see, these German bombers had been going over every night for quite some time to bomb Barrow, but one night they turned and just circled us before dropping their load. We were under the stone slabs in the old pantry and it was absolutely terrifying. The blast blew the front door in and loosened some of our barn doors. We had a mare that was due to foal and she just galloped round and round the field. The foal was born that night and fortunately was all right.

However, one person was killed in the village and four houses were demolished by this five-hundred-pound bomb that landed right in the middle of the road. Other bombs fell on the shore and surrounding fields. The plane also dropped about twenty-five thousand incendiary bombs, which the local schoolchildren collected the tails from over the next few days. We were without all the services, gas, sewerage, water and electricity,

DEFENCE REGULATIONS

IMPORTANT ANNOUNCEMENT

BILLETING

The Government have announced that the dispersal of people in priority classes from certain large towns shall be put into effect immediately.

The area covered by the...........**GRANGE**...................Council is a reception area* to which some of these people are being brought.

Occupiers of housing property in this area are required by law to provide accommodation for any persons assigned to them by the Billeting Officer. Every effort will be made to spread the burden of billeting fairly and equally between households.

It may be necessary to carry out billeting at night as well as day-time. Your co-operation in this emergency is requested.

An allowance will be paid to occupiers for the accommodation provided. To claim this you will need a billeting allowance order form. Watch the bottom of this notice for further information about how to obtain the form.

CLERK OF THE COUNCIL

*If only part of the area is scheduled as a reception area, the districts affected are shown below:

Instructions for obtaining billeting allowance order form:

and what a problem that was for quite some time.

A local lady, Mary Brockbank, wrote some humorous poetry about the villagers' reaction to the bombing, which we all enjoyed. Later, she did more poetry about the arrival of the evacuees. We didn't have any evacuees on the farm as we didn't have enough room with myself, two younger brothers and parents. But there was a load of evacuees came from Acton in

London to the village. They couldn't understand what we were talking about and we couldn't understand them at first. However, there was no problems and they fitted in very well. Incidentally, one of the evacuees came back here after she graduated as a teacher. She was married and had a family by that time and taught in the village school.

After war was declared, the Ministry (of Agriculture) tied you up with everything. How much land you had to plough, how many potatoes you had to grow, the price of calves and sheep. These were controlled and they stayed the same price for years. I remember we used to get twenty-five shillings for every calf, or thirty shillings for the really good ones. You were allowed to keep twenty-five hens yourself, but like lots of farmers, these were kept in the farmyard and others were away in the fields somewhere else. Locals had their share of eggs, even the local bobby.

Milk was taken to Libby's factory at Milnthorpe who canned it for the troops. It was mainly local hauliers who picked these great, big ten-gallon churns up. Ours was K.Fell's, but other areas had their own hauliers. When Libby's used to get a surplus of milk that they couldn't deal with, they

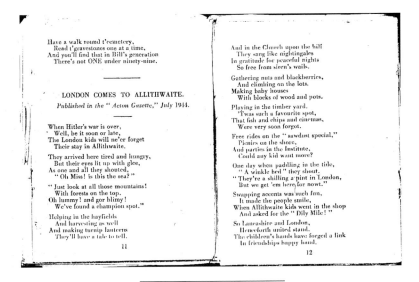

Mary Brockbank's poetry

would send it back rejected the next day. They couldn't cope with it all, and of course, they couldn't get more labour. There was always milk rejected with the 'flush', that's when the cattle went out to grass, in May or June. So what my dad did, and I'm sure that quite a few other farmers did too, they always used to buy pigs in March or April. Then these pigs would use up all the milk that came back from Libby's a couple of months later.

We were killing a pig one night and I was keeping 'nixs' when I saw this light. It was coming along the road and I knew it was a bike as it was the only thing that would have such a small light. So Dad and me kept quiet and locked the door. The following day, the policeman paid us a visit and said to my dad, "I thought there'd been a murder here last night. I could see blood running out from the barn door and I began to be suspicious. But I knew it was your door, so everything would be all right." So the bobby had to have a ham, of course.

The one bobby that comes to mind was called 'Blackout Joe'. You used to have these blinds, blackout ones because of the aeroplanes. This guy used to go round, and any chink of light and he was knocking on the door. But the local police did have problems round here, although there was the military police as well. The bobbies sometimes had a job controlling the forces. Particularly the Americans and Canadians, as they weren't too popular with the British troops. Often there were skirmishes between the Americans and Canadian airmen and the British army lads down in the army camp.

The great problem here was, the Americans had so much more money than the English lads. It wouldn't have been so bad if they'd kept quiet about it. But you know, they used to boast about it so much and that didn't go down very well. So the local bobby was active trying to keep order among the troops and would sometimes get his come-upance. The military police didn't tend to bother with the troops until there was a fracas. Then the ordinary police would ring the camp and out they'd come. And the military police didn't half rough handle anyone who was misbehaving. Oh yes, they showed no quarter at all.

During this time, I was going to Ulverston Grammar School and you travelled with your gas mask every day. It took an hour by bus to Ulverston, so we would be setting off at quarter to eight in the morning and it was quarter to five when you got back at night. They had school meals then and I can remember one significant feature about them. They were very short of milk. When they served semolina pudding, we used to spin the plates around and the semolina wouldn't come off the plate, it was so thick and practically milkless.

I was always expected to help on the farm before and after school and at weekend. What's now a nursing home in Grange-Over-Sands was at the time a convalescent home. Every morning I'd take the milk there, catching the quarter-past seven bus, which would drop me off at the gate. I'd carry the milk to the home and catch another bus back to Allithwaite, where my mother would meet me at the Square. She'd hand me my school bag, take

*American Ambulance Refreshment Trailer. The Furness area was part of the
Lancashire Constabulary's Lonsdale North Police Division. The officer is
Superintendent Parker who headed the Division from Ulverston until 1946.
(The photographs were donated to the Cumbria Police Museum by
Mrs R Albertine who had connectios with the area.)*

the churns off me, and I'd catch the bus to Ulverston. When I came home from school, Mother would meet me with more milk cans and I'd catch a bus to the home, then another bus back to Allithwaite. This all fitted in because the buses ran about every half-hour. I knew all the bus drivers anyhow, and if I was a bit short of time, they'd wait for me.

The home at Grange was mainly for miners from the North East. There would be about seventy of them at a time staying there. They'd been working long and hard hours in the pits and suffered a lot. So they used to come over here for a fortnight's convalescence to recover. Most of them were suffering from chest complaints and coming to the home was the only holiday they'd ever had. They contributed a shilling a week to a club that sent them over here and were given two pounds for a fortnight's spending money. As they queued every night for the local pub to open, that wouldn't last long. None of them wanted to go back to the North East.

In 1944 my Dad broke his ankle, and as we only had one farm man, I left school. The farm-hand we had was Sam Scott from Allithwaite. He was a real character and a hard working man too. Wonderful and witty. "Have you got a new horse, Sammy?" asked one lady. "No, it's t'old one done up," he said. "So and so's cat got run over last week," he was told. "It'll larn it a lesson for running across the road," was Sam's reply. There was a lot of grain grown, mainly oats. Barley wasn't so significant then, it was mainly wheat. All the wheat that was grown, it was examined and had to go to the Ministry. This poor chap from the Ministry had to go round and tell people how much they had to plough. He used to come and measure to see how much you ploughed and oh, he was most unpopular.

Everybody helped one another on the farms because it used to take twelve to fourteen people to thresh. I can always remember a big farm not so very far from here, and I did a whole week there. From half-past seven in the morning to five at night. By Friday night I could hardly lift my arms and shoulders. I was only fifteen then. Same with ploughing. My dad set me off to plough when I was only fifteen on stony scrub land that we'd converted. I ploughed with a mare and its foal that had just been broken in about a month before. I could hardly lie in bed that night because of my shoulders. They worked you hard in them days.

With all that work, you were too tired to go socialising at night. Saturday night was about the limit. You could go to the pictures at Grange but you had to queue because of all the air force and army. Same with the few dances, there'd be plenty of troops there.

At sixteen I joined the Home Guard at Allithwaite. This was run by mostly ex-army, First World War people and my goodness, they were real strict. Nearly all the available men and young lads like myself were in the Home Guard. We used to do training on two nights a week and one night a week on guard duty. What we call Kirkhead Folly, we used to go on duty up there at night. There was all these look-out stations set out all round the area. You know, vantage points so you could use your field glasses and keep a look out over Morecambe Bay. I expect that was to see if the Germans came up Morecambe Bay in a rowing boat.

Some nights we'd practise with our guns and I remember my sten gun jammed. One of the blokes from World War One said, "Oh, I know what's up with it," and took it off me. He didn't make sure it was on 'safe', just grabbed it off me and it went off. The gun was firing into this rock and nearly took my foot with it. He didn't half get told off about that.

We weren't really given instructions about what to do if the Germans landed. Some in the Home Guard were involved with communications. You

Bill

know, passing on messages. There were separate telephone wires to different houses were people in charge lived. Sergeants and people like that. Otherwise, you just were told to wait for instructions and never actually told what you'd have to do. Anyhow, we were too small in number to do much.

When VE and VJ Day came, there were celebrations and relief. But for a considerable time after, food and everything else was still rationed. On looking back, very little was revealed during the war. There was only the radio, so you learnt a lot more after the war was finished than you ever did when it was going on.

*Ted, a retired farmer, is a widower with a family
and Chairman of Allithwaite council.*

NINETEEN

'It always seemed to be raining'

∽

Philip Foxton Craggs, *born 1931 at Hessle, near Hull.*

A s I was getting older, my parents thought I ought to go away and get properly educated. They sent me away to a school locally, but I was at home at Hessle when the war broke out.

My family, and my father in particular, knew the Lake District and liked it. We used to go to Ullswater fairly frequently. As you know, things became very serious with regard to the war in 1940 and my father sent my mother and me to Ullswater. He couldn't come as he was working in a shipyard at Goole.

It was a complicated journey to Ullswater but I don't think it was particularly difficult. We came by train and we certainly had to change at Leeds and Carnforth. We changed somewhere else, but how we got to the nearest station to Ullswater I really don't know.

There was an hotel we knew, the old Ullswater Hotel, and we stayed there for some time. We knew the owners, a family called Bowness, and there was a bit of a family connection. It was an excellent hotel with very high standards and beautifully run. Of course, nowadays, this would be considered austere; in those days such things were considered very important. There were glorious gardens going down to the lake and we were very lucky to be able to stay.

Some of the other guests at the Ullswater Hotel just stayed for the summer months. Others, like us, lived there as a home. There was a major who'd been in the Indian Army and two women who we were very friendly with. And in the evenings we all used to play games, games with letters. It was a great time for card games. There was no television or wireless and we used to entertain ourselves and kept to a very strict timetable.

Obviously there were restrictions because of the war, but it was very much the usual hotel food of the time that we had. Meals were at strict times but there was nothing peculiar about that. I can remember two Burmese wooden figures of men holding up the gong. At meal-times the gong was vigorously beaten. You had to turn up on time or else you didn't get the soup. Brown Windsor soup. Symmington's soup out of a packet, if you're old enough to remember that. There was very little or no choice on the menu. I liked the hotel very much. However, my parents thought of this as a temporary situation.

My mother was born in France, and a French national. As this was the time of the fall of France, it must have been very strange for her to accept that her country had fallen to the enemy. My mother' sister was in France and my grandmother, as it turned out was one of those who left Paris for the West of France in the Exodus. That was when the German troops were advancing rapidly towards the city. My mother received a letter from her mother – her last letter – and the French authorities had written 'DECEASED' across it. Though my mother coped well, it must have been a difficult time for her. But at my age, that was life. Little boys of that age accept a great deal.

Is
YOUR CHILD
away from you
?

WINTER in the country is cold and bleak. Town children exposed for the first time to biting winds and damp mists are very liable to go down with coughs, colds and chills.

See that your child has a jar of Vick brand Vapour-Rub with him. A rub with Vick is the ideal treatment for all children's colds. Children like it and can easily treat themselves at the first sneeze.

You simply rub Vick on the throat, chest and back at bedtime. The salve draws out tightness and breathing becomes easy as the child inhales the healing vapours. By morning, nearly always, the worst of the cold is over.

Post a jar to your child today. Obtainable from all chemists, price 1/3 and *double size* 2/-.

Anyway, I remember being packed-off to school on a daily basis along the road to Glenridding. I used to walk along the lake shore of Ullswater by myself to school. It always seemed to be raining and the rooks were cawing in the trees. To tell you the truth, I haven't the vaguest idea if I took sandwiches with me. Possibly we think more about food than we did in those days. Food was important, but we didn't discuss it quite so much.

There were other children at school who were also from away. I think there was quite a lot of them, so I wasn't a particularly strange being. I know we had to learn some poetry off by heart. But there was a lot of changes at the time and it was a state of great upheaval. There was a lead mine at Ullswater and people were worried about it being bombed. I think at one stage, one bomb did fall on or near the lead mine. It was a curious time. Full of rumours. A time when people were in transit of movement and they were prepared to accept changes.

I had four half-brothers and yes, we did keep in touch and see each other. Three worked in the shipyards, in reserved occupations. One up at Newcastle, one at Hull and the other at Goole. My fourth brother was in the air force and ended up in Gibraltar. I know the shipyard at Goole was kept extremely busy during the war and my father couldn't visit us very often. He certainly did come but there were restrictions on petrol, you see, and his chauffeur was in the forces.

My mother and I would stay at the Ullswater Hotel for about three months. By the time I'd learnt the poem, 'TheBurial of Sir John Moore' at school, my parents were able, with difficulty, to rent a house at Grasmere and we moved there. The house was up by the Swan Hotel at Grasmere and was much more satisfactory.

The House belonged to a Mrs Nichols, who moved into the Swan Hotel. Her house was pleasant, though it was slightly too big for just the two of us. We were allowed to have all the rooms except the drawing room. I remember being shown this room, and I was very excited to see it because it had some oriental antiques. I think Mrs Nichols, the owner, must have had some connection with the Far East, as she had some fire-screens and so on, with elaborate carvings. As this room was locked up, Mother and me spent most of our time in the morning room and the kitchens. But it was all the Lake District at Grasmere and I liked it very much.

PATTERDALE'S FOOD SUPPLY.

Will Still Come from Penrith.

At Thursday's meeting of the Lakes Urban Council at Ambleside, Mr. A. Walton stated that they were "in the dark" at Patterdale in reference to food control arrangements, and he asked for some information. At present most of their food came from Penrith. What would happen if they were strictly rationed? Would they have to get some of the food from over the Pass (Kirkstone)? No one seemed to know much about it.

The Clerk (Mr. Sowerby) said the whole of the food control business up to the outbreak of war was a secret. Even the officers themselves did not know very much. Patterdale would be able to get their food supplies from the same place from which they previously had supplies.

The Council decided to proceed with certain of its house building schemes, including that at Glenridding.

Plans were approved for overhead electricity lines at Deepdale and Hartsop for the Westmorland Electricity Company subject to a plan of the agreed line being submitted.

Plans were passed for the drainage system of King George's Field.

But wherever we were during the war years, my parents and I had maps from newspapers, with arrows showing the course of the war and various fronts. I listened to Mr Churchill's broadcasts and the wireless reports avidly, as we all did. My father never swore, but when he heard of the concentration camps and the extermination of the Jews, his horrified reaction about the Nazis was, "Oh blast them. Blast them." in good North Country fashion.

In due time I was sent to a school that had evacuated from Leeds. This was at a big house, The Hollins at Grasmere, which is now the headquarters of the National Trust in the North West. I remember walking

WESTMORLAND AS A RECEPTION AREA

The county of Westmorland is generally famous as being the home of the Lake District, but this popular and well-known part is a comparatively small area lying round the main road from Kendal through Windermere to Keswick; this part of the county contains mostly hotels, boarding-houses, and large private houses. The county extends to half-a-million acres and is mainly agricultural with scattered villages; the only town of any size is Kendal (pre-war population circ. 17,000) which has some factories and is the main market town for two-thirds of the county. The climate is mild with a heavy rainfall. The people are sturdy, independent and self-reliant; most villages maintain their own clubs, sporting, dramatic, etc. Often bus routes are remote with infrequent services, and some valleys have very little contact with the outside world. Nonconformity has always flourished in Westmorland which is, indeed, one of the original homes of Quakerism. There was little poverty in the county, and with a few exceptions the housing conditions were good. The summer visitors were attracted by mountaineering, fishing and the beauties of Nature, and did not come in search of such entertainments as popular seaside resorts provide. It follows that such visitors were on the whole of a social class rather different from the slum dwellers of the big cities and this made the contrast with the evacuees much accentuated.

FROM HOME & EUROPE 1939-1949
J F DOW MD, MARJORIE A BROWN MA,
PUBLISHED BY WESTMORLAND GAZETTE

to school and seeing the little becks coming down the fellside. I used to have lunch at home and before I got back to my mother, I played with these becks, damming them up. Oh, I really enjoyed that. That's what I remember most of all.

We were more or less all 'foreigners' at the school. I've got to repeat, small boys accepted things at that time. We accepted our lives were full of surprises and full of changes. I was certainly not unhappy. "Am I happy?", was not something that crossed my mind. Perhaps nowadays people ask themselves a great deal, and I don't think we did in those days. The country was under dire threat and people made the most of things.

Oh yes, we went in the village as you bought things locally in those days. If you were lucky they were delivered once a week during the war. We went to J.J. Foster, the grocer. Mr Foster was the village grocer and it was then we must have became rather friendly. In the course of time, his sister became one of the best friends I've ever had in my life.

Socially, I concentrated more on school and my mother joined the local Women's Institute. You know about the W.I. of course. It was a great thing, especially during the war. Preservation of food, making jams and so on.

After a while I was put down for a school in Warwickshire that my father knew, so we moved back down to Yorkshire. I stayed at school in Warwickshire until the end of the war. After the war, we came back up here, to Grasmere. Mr Foster, the grocer we were talking about, sold us a piece of land, and I think we've still got the plans for a house that was never built. Later on, my mother lived in a house called The Close at Grasmere, as she liked the area very much. Finally she went to live in London, which was much easier for her.

When Anthea and I married and lived in London we had a little house at Easedale, which is to the north-west of Grasmere. When our tenant died, we had to come back to settle things and I got a job as a teacher at a school called Heighton Hill just below Ambleside. That's how my teaching career began. All this came about through our connections with Grasmere during the war years.

My mother's sister survived the war in France, but my father's chauffeur is dead now. We're still very friendly with his family and they've been to stay with us. My last remaining brother died recently, so we've lost a lot of information which would have been very interesting. You see, the shipyard at Goole where my father worked was sold after the war. I'm sure they did work on the Mulberry Harbour, which was useful at the landings in Normandy. I really do wish I knew more about this.

Married with a family, Philip is a semi-retired teacher.

TWENTY

'Call out the Home Guard'

∽

Joe Hawes, was born at Skelsmergh near Kendal, but has lived for the last seventy-two years at Docker. ,

He was a dothering old bugger, was Chamberlain. Well, the way he went across to Germany and then he came back again. He said this, that and t'other and the next thing we were at war. They should have had old Churchill there at the very start. He would have sorted them out. Oh yes, the way things were, you could weight it up, like. You could tell there would be a war.

I went into farm service when war was declared. That was at Austerwick, over Ingleton side. I went to work for my auntie. She'd wrote to my mother, saying "Joe's leaving school. Can he come over?" Worst bloody job I ever did, working for relations.

Half-a-crown a week and my food I had at Ingleton. All sorts I did. Milking, mucking out and scaling shit. And the family were undertakers as well as farmers. I used to get into the hearse and polish that. Polish the old brasses, all the horse gear and the horse shoes. It was an old army horse from the First World War they had for pulling the hearse. It still had all sorts of military numbers clipped into its buttocks. I tell you, every time they had a funeral, they had Joe cleaning the hearse out.

Oh, it was a real carriage do for a funeral. It was a nice turnout, I can tell you, when everything was polished up. Then there was matey (the driver) in a jacket and top hat and with his whip. We'd take the hearse down to the door, load it up with the coffin, and away we went. Oh, it was good, it was.

We had the Ministry (of Agriculture) round telling us what to do and what we hadn't to do on the farm. So much to plough, get more stock (animals) and all this carry-on. And then the subsidies came. You were nobbut allowed to keep two pigs if you weren't a pigbreeder. You see, it worked out that if you had two pigs, one had to go for somebody else's ration and you were only allowed to keep one for yourself. You had to apply to the Ministry if you were going to butch a pig. The Ministry would come round and you didn't know if they were Ministry men or bloody hooks (crooks). That was done many a time. "Oh, I believe you have two pigs? Well, we've got to take one." You never heard no more about it. Bloody hooks. But there was many that kept two or three pigs. You know, black market job, and were raking it (money) in left, right and centre.

We had a Reading Room next door to the farm. So, lad-like, I used to go there every night for a game of darts at half-penny a game. And this auntie would say, "Leave them lasses alone." Oh, by God, if she thought you were talking to a lass, that was a hell of a crime. "Aye, don't start messing about with them or else I'll tell yer mother," I was told.

After my six months' service was up, auntie said, "Are you coming back here?" "Oh, aye," I told her, but when I got on that bloody bus, I thought, "Well, that's the finish of Ingleton and they're not getting me back." Off I went back home to Docker and went to work for an old lad.

Well, that was a bigger farm and I had more to do. Mind, it was a hungry bloody spot. It's a wonder we never had bloody lugs (ears) like rabbits' cos of all the lettuce we used to eat. And pilchards. Oh, every Friday pilchards for dinner. The old lad and his missus used to go to Kendal in the horse and cart every Friday. They made a day of it to see the market and all that carry-on. And it was always a tin of pilchards left for my dinner. I'd say to the maid, "What's for dinner today, Renee?" and the answer always was, "Pilchards". "Put an egg on top for me, Renee. I can't live off these things." I'd tell her. She used to pop a boiled egg on with the pilchards and that would fill me up a bit.

The old lad and another farmer used to both come across to our house every night. They came to listen to the news on the wireless every night all through the war years. Then came the night when it was announced that France had capitulated. Well, I've never seen owt like that old farmer. That was it, with him. "Let them sheep out, Joe. Let them out. They'll (Germans) be here." He lost all heart in everything.

It would be about that time, a family business evacuated from Kent to up here (Kendal). They moved all the family up and stayed in a spare building belonging to an uncle and auntie. Well, many a night I'd bike down to see them. They never gave you a cup of tea, it was always drink. Pimms No.1. Jesus Christ, you've got to be tough to stand drink like that every night. As soon as you got in the room, the bottle was on the table and loads of meat. I'd get tanked up and try to bike home at two o'clock in the morning. Many a time on the way home, I'd think, "Bugger it," and fall asleep on a pile of them little stones by the side of the roadside they used for tarring roads. I'd have my old bike on top of me and somebody always woke me up the next day.

I joined the Home Guard. Brush shaft and a bit of string with crackers on, like jumping jacks. That's all we had. Tied the crackers onto the string, pulled the string, and pop, pop. It made a noise like a gun. Eventually we got rifles. No ammunition, that came later. And then we got our uniforms.

Bomb Damage at Cooper House, Selside

Our job was to guard the railway viaduct up here as that was the main railway line up to Scotland. We used to go way up the line as far as Lowgill checking up. In our pockets we had these detonators. We were supposed to run up the line and put these detonators on if the Germans came. And that was it. We hadn't a cat in hell's chance if owt did happen.

I was on duty the night Cooper House at Selside went up (17 April 1941). There was three of us on the viaduct and we could hear this droning coming. Then there was hundreds of bloody incendiary bombs. You could have stood on the viaduct and read a paper. After that we heard one almighty thud and we thought, "Hell, somebody has gone up." As time went on, another three bombs were dropped right across the bottom of the fell. All the sheep and cows starting bawling and carrying on. I tell you, talk about shaking on that bloody viaduct. I did that night.

Folk reckoned there was a convoy going up the A6 (Shap Fell) at the time of the bombing. There wasn't, the convoy had already gone. The plane had missed it, he was too bloody late. But because of the incendiary bombs, the place was all lit up just like Blackpool. If he had come further along, he would have seen the viaduct and bombed that.

Oh, a lot of trains came up this way, as it was the main line. Trains full of ammunition and troops on the move. Same with the A6 up Shap Fell. Convoys and convoys were going up there and civilian lorries. And in winter, there would be accidents one after another. That bloody beck bottom, it used to be littered with wagons that had gone through the wall.

One dark night, an old lad in the Home Guard came out of the signal box near the viaduct. He had a great (long) bayonet, double-barrel shot gun, a crook in one hand and carrying an umbrella in the other. Over his shoulder was his bait bag. He came out at the end of the viaduct and there was sic (such) a bang. By God, he turned round and ran back again shouting, "Call them out. Call out the Home Guard. There's been a shot fired." He was in such a state, he swung his bait bag round and discovered it was his pop (lemonade) bottle top that had blown off.

Then one night, there was some prisoners got away from Shap Wells (Prisoner-of-War Camp) and everybody was warned about them. A right farm lad was coming up the lane towards the crossings when he sees these two figures sitting on some railings. "Good neet." he says, and walks on up to the crossings box where there was one or two of the Home Guard inside. After a bit they said to this lad, "Have you seen anybody on your travels." Well, it was the two that matey spoke to. Of course, these two prisoners had gone when they went to look for them, but they were caught at Oxenholme. So you can tell what the Home Guard was like.

LONDON MIDLAND AND SCOTTISH RAILWAY COMPANY
(WESTERN DIVISION).

THIS TIME TABLE MUST BE KEPT STRICTLY PRIVATE, AND MUST NOT BE GIVEN TO THE PUBLIC.

WORKING TIME TABLE
OF
PASSENGER TRAINS NOTICE.

SECTIONS 1, 2, 3, & 4.

JULY 1st 1940 until further notice.

THE WORKING TIME TABLE OF PASSENGER TRAINS (Sections 1, 2, 3 and 4, dated January 1st, 1940, also Oxheys, Preston and Euxton Junction, dated February 5th, 1940), will, with the alterations and additions included herein, remain in operation until further notice.

SECTION 2. (Also Oxheys, Preston and Euxton Jn.)
WORKMEN'S SERVICES — WEEK-ENDS.
The following altered and additional arrangements will operate each week-end, on the respective days, until further notice :—

12.33 a.m. (MX) fish, Carlisle to Manchester (Ex.), is "Q." (8–6–40)
2.12 a.m. (MX) parcels, Carlisle to Manchester (Ex.), retimed from Penrith, pass 2.44, Shap Summit 3.13, Tebay 3.14, Oxenholme 3.36, Carnforth arr. 3.48, dep. 4.2, Lancaster pass 4.11, Garstang & C. 4.31, Oxheys 4.34, Preston arr. 4.41 a.m. (4 minutes recovery time, Oxheys to Preston.) (Commencing 2–7–40)
6. 5 a.m., Carlisle to Crewe, retimed ; Southwaite 6.19, dep. 6.20, Calthwaite 6.26, Plumpton arr. 6.32, dep. 6.33, Penrith arr. 6.41, dep. 6.47, Shap arr. 7.8, dep. 7.9, Shap Summit pass 7.13, Tebay arr. 7.20, dep. 7.23, Low Gill arr. 7.30, dep. 7.32, Grayrigg arr. 7.36, dep. 7.37, Oxenholme arr. 7.52, dep. 7.57 p.m., forward unaltered. (Commencing 1–7–40)
6.40 a.m. Sundays, Carlisle to Barrow, ceases to call at Curthwaite. (17–3–40)
New empty stock leaves Carlisle (Citadel) 7.0 a.m. for Carlisle (No. 12), arr. 7.3 a.m. (Conveys stock off 10.55 p.m. from Euston.) (3–2–40)
7.10 a.m. Sundays, Carlisle to Whitehaven (Bransty), ceases to call at Curthwaite. (17–3–40)
New empty stock leaves Carlisle (Citadel) 8.5 a.m. Sundays for Carlisle (No. 12), arr. 8.8 a.m. (Conveys Postal vans.) (4–2–40)
8.35 a.m. H. & C., Carlisle to Crewe, is "passenger," Southwaite to Oxenholme, daily. (3–2–40)
9. 0 a.m., 9.15 a.m., 12.0 noon (SO), 8.40 p.m. (SO), 10.35 p.m., 11.15 p.m. empty stock trains, Carlisle (Citadel) to Carlisle (No. 12), discontinued. (3–2–40)
New empty stock leaves Carlisle (Citadel) 9.30 a.m. for Carlisle (No. 12), arr. 9.33 a.m. (Conveys stock off 8.3 a.m. from Penrith, 6.10 a.m. from Kilmarnock, and 7.40 a.m. from Appleby (TFO).) (3–2–40)
1.25 p.m. empty stock, Carlisle (No. 12 Box) to Carlisle (Citadel), leaves at 1.35 p.m., Citadel arr. 1.38 p.m., and conveys stock to work 2.0 p.m. to Oxenholme, not Morecambe. (22–1–40)
New empty stock departs Carlisle (Citadel) 1.50 p.m. for Carlisle (No. 12), arr. 1.53 p.m. (off 9.27 a.m. from Crewe). (20–5–40)
3.50 p.m. Sundays (milk), Carlisle to Euston, calls at Milnthorpe and is retimed ; Oxenholme pass 3.5, Milnthorpe arr. 5.14, dep. 5.20, Carnforth pass 3.30, Lancaster 5.37, Garstang & C. 5.51, Oxheys 6.1, Preston 6.9 p.m. (26–5–40)
New empty stock departs Carlisle (No. 12) 3.57 p.m. Sundays for Carlisle (Citadel), arr. 4.0 p.m. (To work 8.35 p.m. to Euston, also P.O. vans.) (4–2–40)
4. 0 p.m. Sundays, Carlisle to Whitehaven (Bransty), ceases to call at Dalston and Curthwaite. (17–3–40)
4. 5 p.m. (milk), Carlisle to Euston, calls at Milnthorpe, retimed ; Carlisle dep. 4.5, Plumpton pass 4.35, Penrith 4.39, Shap Summit 5.9, Tebay 5.7, Oxenholme 5.31, Milnthorpe arr. 5.29, dep. 5.35, Carnforth pass 5.44, Lancaster 5.52, Garstang & Catterall 5.07, Oxheys 6.16, Preston 6.18 p.m. (27–5–40)
New empty stock departs Carlisle (No. 12) 4.30 p.m. for Carlisle (Citadel) arr. 4.33 p.m. (To work 4.55 p.m. to Penrith.) (20–5–40)

143

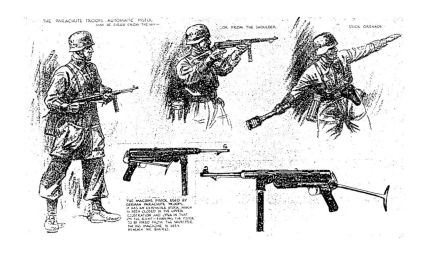

How to engage parachute troops

---

1. The parachutist is most vulnerable just when he alights and before he has had time to release his parachute and harness, re-adjust his belt outside his overalls, and open the container and get hold of his real weapons. For the space of about 30 seconds, therefore, he is not a very formidable enemy as he is unlikely to have weapons except two or three hand grenades and an automatic pistol with a limited range. As soon as the men have opened the containers and retrieved their weapns they become very formidable opponents.

2. The first duty of those who observe a parachute descent is to warn the police or military authorities, and to observe the actions of the enemy. But where resistance can be offered it will be most effective in the brief interval after the men have alighted, and every effort should be made to keep them fom reaching their containers. This can be done either by fire directed at the parachutists or by firing at the containers themselves.

3. The containers are very vulnerable to small arms fire, either from rifles or light machine guns. Packed as they are with loaded weapons, hand grenades, ammunition and possible explosives, a great deal of damage can be done to them by bursts of fire from rifles or light machine guns.
   If the parchutists have been killed, or if containers are found unopened, then the weapons in them might be of much use to the defenders, especially in view of the possibility that the parachutists are the forerunners of air-borne troops. A knowledge of these weapons is therefore essential.

THE WAR OFFICE
June 1940.

Oh, some right comics we had. It was a wonder nobody was killed. There was one lad and when he got hold of a rifle, he shut both eyes and pulled the trigger. There was sods flying everywhere. Then we went down to Gatebeck to practise with hand-grenades. Oh man, that bloody lad shouldn't have been allowed there. He was frightened to death and the NCO (non commissioned officer) was with him, watching every move he made. This lad pulled the pin out of the grenade and he let go of it. Matey (NCO) clicked (caught) it and threw it over the wall. If he hadn't, there would have been a few of us gone that day.

Mind, some of them NCOs like, they thought they were the cat's whiskers. I don't doubt it among a lot of farm lads. One NCO was a dothering old bugger. It was, "Well men, you know when it happens, (the invasion), I want you to be prepared," and all this bloody carry-on. Us prepared, and still with bloody broom shafts? Still, you saw some blokes coming with larl (little) parcels for the NCO's and gaffers. Bacon and eggs they had in the parcels. That's how they got their corporal's stripes, you see. Bacon-and-egg stripes we called them.

In the Home Guard, we used to meet at the farm house next door, Thompson's of Docker Hall. We'd go into the house and sit down on the chairs and wait for instructions. Well, one night I got there, got sat down and lit a fag. "Private Hawes", says the Sergeant, "get that cigarette out." "Right, that's the bloody finish," I thought, and joined Grayrigg Village Hall lot. That was a lot better. A lot of younger lads there.

In country districts Incendiary Bombs will be used extensively because they are cheap, light to carry and intensely destructive. This is the opinion of experts.

Magnesium (Electron) Bombs will start many fires but they can be effectively dealt with in the early stages by a suitable hand pump with a JET TO PUT OUT THE FIRE and a SPRAY TO COOL DOWN THE BOMB and make it burn away in a few moments (See A.R.P. Handbook No. 9).

You cannot afford to be without a STIRRUP PUMP and several buckets of water in your upper floor. When peace comes, we will beat our swords into ploughshares and stirrup pumps will be used for spraying roses.

Insure your house and your roses by ordering a STIRRUP PUMP with DUAL JET OR SPRAY NOZZLE and 30 feet of hose (Delivery from stock or in a few days).

Price Complete

35/-

NETT.

DISCOUNT FOR QUANTITIES.

Gilbert Gilkes & Gordon, Ltd., Kendal
TEL. KENDAL 28

Mind, I had to go out spick and span for the Home Guard. Because of my father, you see. He'd been through the First World War and knew what was what. Every button had to be spot on or he'd say, "You're not going out like a bloody tramp." But every so often we had a church Parade and oh, deary me. We'd all line up and there'd be hay seeds on great-coats and cowshit on shoes. Folk worked in their uniform all week.

My father was working for the council during the daytime and a special constable at nights all round this area. There was plenty doing for him with them bloody farm lads. You know what lads are like. One night there was a field of corn all set up to dry and a gang of lads had gone and sorted it all out. So the bogies (police) were round the next morning and eventually these lads were fined thirty bob each.

No, I wasn't with them that night. I was in the other job when we hid part of a fella's plough. He never did find out because we buried it. And the old fella (Father), he quizzed and quizzed for long enough about that but I never made him any wiser. I'd have got the belt if he'd found out, even at my age.

I wanted to join up and my dad was all for it. I went down to Kendal to join but they wouldn't have me because I was on the land. "Stop where you're at. You're needed there," I was told. But I was disappointed. Folk looked at you and said, "Oh aye, hiding on the bloody land?" and all this, you know. Which wasn't so. We did our best to get in the forces but they wouldn't have us.

One night when I was at home, there was a plane came down low. Me and Mother were standing at the gate watching it. "Bloody hell, he's low. He's going to get us," I thought. The pilot had landing lights on but he went away and kept coming back and circling round and round. There's a farm up yonder (New Hutton) and he went straight up those fields, getting shot (rid) of his bombs near Fisher Tarn. The pilot went nearly to Sedbergh Road at Kendal before he came to a standstill. They were our lads (British) who had got engine trouble and were lost. That road was closed for weeks and weeks.

Well, when that plane was going round and round, everybody was tensed up at home. We didn't know what was going on. Once over when the plane went away, everything was quiet. Then my sister heard these feet outside come pitter-patter, pitter-patter. She grabbed a pitchfork and said, "If the buggers come here, I'll chuck (throw) this fork through them." Then the feet stopped and all was quiet and we heard "Baaaaahhh." It was a bloody sheep coming down the road and it stopped at our gate. My sister had thought it was the Germans coming.

Oh Christ, we seen enough of them Eyeties (Italians). They weren't very good workers but some of them stayed on farms and folk even took them to the bloody pictures. And our (local) lasses were keen on them, by God they were. Army wagons used to take these Eyeties to work on the farms and come to collect them when they had finished for the day. A few of us came across about six of these army wagons one day that had come to collect the Eyeties. So we let their tyres down. Oh, they were looked after and it made you sick when you were just on a push-bike.

Well, the war finished and then came the winter of '47. That was a bad carry-on. We were snowed up to the lug-holes here. Blokes were digging for ages to clear the roads. My mother made buckets of tea for them all day long and give them apple pasties. Like bloody wolves they were, that hungry with all that work. But still, everything got over with and we had some good laughs through the war years. We had some good moments. By God, we did.

Joe, a married man is a retired farm labourer and lorry driver. He is Chairman of Docker Parish Meeting, President of Grayrigg Sports Committee and on the committees for the Coronation Hall and Grayrigg Alms Houses.

TWENTY ONE

'That was called using initiative'

∽

*Peter Yuile, born Croydon in 1926 but moved to
Barrow-in-Furness in 1929.*

I lost my mother in 1929. She died as a result of an operation for tonsillitis, which was a major operation in those days. My father remarried a widow in '35 who had two sons. Both these sons went into the forces before the war. The older one joined the Militia, the very first conscription in 1939. He was supposed to be conscripted for six months but it was six years later when he came out. The younger one, who was four years older than myself, he was lost on 25 November 1941. That was on HMS Barham in the Mediterranean, when she got four torpedoes and her magazines blew up. Eight hundred and sixty-eight men were killed on the ship. It's the only Royal Navy ship that has a memorial service held every year at Westminster Abbey. My own brother, who was older then me, went into the army.

I was still at school, Walney Central, when the war broke out. As school children we had to dig trenches there in case any German aircraft landed. Then we had our school allotment and grew vegetables. Out of school, we collected bomb fragments and shrapnel that fell during the Blitz on Barrow. One of the prize finds was the silk cord from the parachute mines.

In 1941 I left school and went to Vickers'. I don't think I had any choice about what I wanted to do. It was a case of you followed your father, and that was it. I sat an entrance exam for an apprenticeship, and in those days you had to be sixteen to start. So, for the remaining months until I was sixteen, I was an office boy, running messages between departments.

There was about twenty thousand people at Vickers' during the war, ship-building, working on the gun side of things, and all sorts. HMS Illustrious and Indomitable were aircraft carriers which were both built at Vickers at the beginning of the war. They were both damaged on the Malta convoys. I can remember working on these guns as an apprentice when they came back for repairs.

Of course we had the Blitz in Barrow, which was mainly from April to May 1941. We'd raids before then and there were raids after, but spring 1941 was the worst time. It seemed as though the planes were over and dropping bombs every night. That's when people started going out into the countryside to sleep.

Bomb damage at Union Street, Barrow-in-Furness

It's very difficult for people to visualise our wartime experiences now. Everybody was in the same boat. At night you had to put your blackouts up and prevent any lights showing. There was no street lighting or anything like that. You were allowed to have a torch with very limited power. Same with bicycles, they had a limited light. Bike mudguards, kerbs, the base of lamp posts and the base of trees near the main road, all had to be painted white so that you could see them at night.

Because I was working in munitions, I couldn't be called up, as it was a reserved occupation. Even if you volunteered, you had a job to get away if you were in a reserved occupation. So I joined the Barrow ATC (Air Training Corps) in September 1941.

The ATC was held at the County Club on the junction of Abbey Road and Hindpool Road. There was about one hundred and fifty of us lads there and Flight Lieutenant Dodd was the Commanding Officer. We used to go three nights a week to the ATC for various lectures and learnt about navigation, Morse code, signalling and all sorts of things. On a Saturday or Sunday we used to go to Haverigg Airfield for flying.

Haverigg Airfield would have over two thousand people stationed and working there. When it first opened, it was called Number Two Bombing and Gunnery School. Then it became Number Two Advanced Observer School. After that, it was Observer (Advanced Flying Unit) still doing the same things throughout the war. It was for navigators doing navigational exercises. There'd be pilots who'd qualified and came to do practice flights or longer flights with a navigator.

I'd say about seventy to eighty per cent of the pilots were RAF and the other twenty per cent could be Canadians, Australians or Polish men. The ones who'd trained in Canada and the States didn't have the weather conditions that we have here, so they came to gain experience. The Americans, especially found it very bad when they came over. You only need to look in Haverigg cemetery and see the graves of the airmen to see that it was a mixed crowd.

RAF Millom, 1941. Left to right. Bill Hickox, Grp Captain Wray, Godfrey Winn, John Archibold and W/Cdr Hadow

In the ATC we did all our first flights in Avro Ansons. At that stage we didn't have an individual log book, only a collective number of hours flown was entered. Quite often the planes were dual-controlled and the pilot would let you fly the craft. Half the time us cadets didn't know where we were going. The pilot might fly to north Wales, over to the Isle of Man, or up to Scotland and back. As it was usually navigational exercise, they mainly had to pinpoint an area where they had to fly to.

WHITEHAVEN NEWS

RAF Millom, 1941

Before going on flight, we had to draw out of the stores a parachute and a 'Mae West'. Do you know what a Mae West was? It was an RAF life vest named after a buxom film star. The parachutes had a fitted harness, which had to be the correct length. Usually the WAAF's showed you how to put it on. But you always had to be careful how you carried these parachutes as, if the D-ring was lifted from the harness, it released the silk, which billowed out. If that happened, you had to pay a fine to the WAAF's slush fund.

In the summer of '43 we spent a week up at Haverigg in tents. During that time we were flying, attending lectures, and all basic training stuff. And we had to do the fatigues. Good fatigues were working in the cookhouse, which was mainly peeling spuds. But the WAAF's took pity on us and it was, "Here you are, have a piece of fruitcake." The fatigues that weren't too pleasant were cleaning the toilets, which were just buckets. This was called the bucket brigade.

When Walney Airfield opened, about four of their officers used to come to the Barrow ATC as instructors. Now, as an apprentice at Vickers, I worked a fortnight on day shifts and a fortnight on night shift. When I was on nights, we used to finish at half-past seven in the morning. Nearly everybody in Barrow had a bicycle for work and there was a rush as hundreds of cyclists came out of Vickers' at the same time.

In summer I'd cycle home, have something to eat and go to Walney ATC. They got to know me at the guard room. I'd go over to the officer in charge of flying, who'd be in the control tower, knock on the door, salute and ask, "Anything I can do, sir?" In the next breath it would be, "Any flying, sir?" He'd answer, "Go over to the hangar and make yourself useful."

Over at the hangar, I'd see the Flight Sergeant and say, "Anything I can do, Flight Sergeant? The OC (Officer in Charge) said I could go flying, if there is any flying." I'd be told, "Well, go and clean the windows of the Avro Anson and make yourself useful." After a while you'd see a pilot with his parachute harness coming over from the parachute store towards the hangar. Well, this aircraft would just be outside the hangar. I'd just cleaned its windows, so it would be going to fly.

The next stage was to approach the pilot and you'd say, "Excuse me, are you going flying?" His reply was usually, "Yes. Are you going up on air test?" I'd answer, "Yes. Can I come with you?" I'd be told to get myself a parachute, and off we'd go. That was called 'using initiative'. You see, in the ATC we were only supposed to go on the airfields or fly as an official party, but I was going as an individual.

By this time, it was approaching D-Day. In the South Lakes there was the 51st Highland Division, which comprised of five of the major Scottish regiments. They camped all round Barrow, Dalton and the Ulverston area. There were loads of camps for these men. Every Saturday morning, their combined pipe band used to play while marching around Barrow. Then, a week before D-Day, the Highland Division disappeared, so we thought, "It's going to be near." I don't think anybody knew exactly when D-Day was going to be, but when the Highlanders suddenly moved out, it was a definite sign.

Just as the Highlanders disappeared, the Americans arrived at Barrow. They'd come straight over from the States, so they were as green as anything. Of course, they had loads of sweets and were always giving them to the youngsters. It was the old story, 'overpaid, over-sexed, and over here'. Their wages were about three times what the British lads were getting.

I'd volunteered for the services in 1944 but it wasn't until the end of '45 that I actually went in the RAF. So the war was all but over by the time I was going in. Anyhow, I did under three years in the RAF and then went back to Vickers'. They had to reinstate you under the Reinstatement Act. Anybody who'd gone into the services during the war, their employer had to take them back. I went back and finished my apprenticeship. But by that time, I'd got used to travel. Also, there were hundreds of thousands coming out of the forces and there wasn't really the work. The armaments side was winding down and peacetime production hadn't got into full swing. So I went away to sea, and spent thirty-eight years at sea as an engineer.

Then five years ago, I heard a Radio Cumbria interview with John Nixon from Haverigg Museum. He'd found the first Anson engine that had been brought ashore from the war years. You see, a lot of planes went down on the fells, and at least five came down in the sea. Very few records were kept of what happened in those days. You'd just find, 'Called out to crashed aircraft', and that's about all that's entered. So it was through listening to the Radio Cumbria interview that I got involved with the Haverigg RAF Museum. Then I passed on all my war-time photographs of Walney to the museum, and we've combined.

Every year we have a reunion for all the people who served at Haverigg. But now, at the reunion, we've also got people attending who were stationed at Walney or Cark. We even had a chap who landed on Lake Windermere where they made the Sunderland flying boats. Well, he lives in Australia, but actually, he's a Walney chap. So it's amazing what's developed in these last five years.

Peter, now a widower, was in the Merchant Navy for thirty-eight years before retiring. He is on the Civilian Committee for the Barrow A.T.C. and a member of RAF Millom Museum (Haverigg).

TWENTY TWO

'For the next five weeks
I peeled potatoes'

∞

*Victor Wilson, born 1925 at Dundee. His wife, Freda, born 1936 at
Lupton but moved to Longsleddale shortly after.*

VICTOR: I joined the army in Aberdeen. Our barracks were very basic
and years later when I learned that the RAF had sheets on their beds, I
couldn't believe it. We just had rough blankets and no pillows. In fact, if
you brought pyjamas from civvie street, they were confiscated.

Whether it was because my father had a haulage business, I don't know,
but after my twelve weeks' basic training, I was sent with some others to
the Royal Army Service Corps at Carlisle. Compared with Aberdeen,
Hadrian's Camp at Carlisle was heaven on earth because everything was
under cover. Spiders, the buildings were called. There was a main room
and all the dormitories, or huts as they were called, led off from there. Oh,
it was Heaven.

That's where I learnt to be a driver, at Carlisle. Most of the fellas could
already drive because in them days, you could drive without having to pass
a test. I'd been driving because of my connection with my father's firm so
I'd only my driving test to pass. Believe it or not, I only travelled about
three inches and I passed the test.

About twelve of us were going for our driving test and we all piled into
this three-ton Bedford truck. There was this sergeant, he was the instructor
and his name was also Wilson. I'll never forget him because when I got
into the cab beside him, he says "Oh, a Driver Wilson. Well, you're not
going to let the side down, are you?" "No Sergeant, " I replied and he said,
"Right, set off."

We were on a bit of an incline on the road and I set off in the prescribed
manner and Sergeant Wilson said, "Stop. In the army, you set off and travel
an inch before you let the hand-brake off," What he meant was, make sure
I didn't run back. So I did what I was told and he said, "Stop. Right, you've
passed. Get in the back of the truck and send the next bloke in." That was
my army test.

Now, we were supposed to be learning to drive for six weeks and I'd
passed my test in the first week. So for the next five weeks I peeled
potatoes. With hindsight, I should have failed the test as I'd have been

gadding about the Lake District with the rest of the lads. So that was it, I just peeled potatoes and did normal guard duty for the next five weeks.

I enjoyed guard duty, which was known as 'picket'. We walked around Hadrian's Camp with a pick-handle because we didn't have guns. There was always one man from each of the seven huts chosen for this duty and we had a special set of boots, gaiters, greatcoat and hat. Everything was especially bulled up (polished) for guard duty. During parade for the guard, one of the seven men from the huts, was picked as the best and he was called 'the stickman'. Now all the stickman did was to go to the canteen and mess hall, get the guards' supper and take it back to the guard room. Then he was finished for the evening. Each of us who were chosen to be the 'stickman' was always quite proud of this. You know, we were young and silly.

Victor (sitting inside the car)
during his army days

155

We all became fully operational drivers at Hadrian's Camp but we also had to be soldiers. Therefore we had to become efficient with guns and went on the rifle ranges, firing rifles, sten guns and bren guns. If you became proficient in all three, I think it was about another threepence a day you got. Our wage was twenty-one shillings a week and everything was all found.

I was only eighteen-and-a-half at that time, and most of the people who I'd joined up with were older. Eventually, there was only me of the original ones left. I don't know if it was a written rule but it was certainly an unwritten rule that you didn't send any soldier abroad until they were nineteen. So I had orders to fill in my time and was sent to a unit at Heaton Hall. From there, we drove these little three-ton chevs which pulled guns up the coast to Wallsend, Morpeth, Newcastle and Haddington. Come night, if there was an air raid, the Royal Artillery fired these guns. I would have stayed there the rest of the time in the army as I enjoyed that so much. But it wasn't to be.

(Victor was sent abroad and served in Air Despatch 7 in India and Waterborne Company in Singapore.)

FREDA: We were living at Stockdale Farm, almost at the top of Longsleddale Valley. Besides my parents and me there was my older brother and sister. We lived in a little world of our own. Us kiddies walked the three miles to school each day and went to Sunday School and that was the only time we saw others of our own age. At home I spent my time fishing or making mud pies.

I think the war passed us by. I mean, we had enough food. We had our own butter, eggs and meat, and we were allowed to kill a pig every year. We used to have hams hanging from the ceiling, and if anybody came for dinner, Mam would lift a ham down, and slice a lump off it. Then the lump of ham would be thrown in the frying-pan with a couple of eggs and the visitor would have a good meal.

'For the next five weeks I peeled potatoes'

REASONS FOR RATIONING

War has meant the re-planning of our food supplies. Half our meat and most of our bacon, butter and sugar come from overseas. Here are four reasons for rationing :—

1 RATIONING PREVENTS WASTE OF FOOD We must not ask our sailors to bring us unnecessary food cargoes at the risk of their lives.

2 RATIONING INCREASES OUR WAR EFFORT Our shipping carries food, and armaments in their raw and finished state, and other essential raw materials for home consumption and the export trade. To reduce our purchases of food abroad is to release ships for bringing us other imports. So we shall strengthen our war effort.

3 RATIONING DIVIDES SUPPLIES EQUALLY There will be ample supplies for our 44½ million people, but we must divide them fairly, everyone being treated alike. No one must be left out.

4 RATIONING PREVENTS UNCERTAINTY Your Ration Book assures you of your fair share. Rationing means that there will be no uncertainty — *and no queues.*

YOUR RATION BOOK IS YOUR PASSPORT TO EASY PURCHASING OF BACON & HAM, BUTTER AND SUGAR

AN ANNOUNCEMENT BY THE MINISTRY OF FOOD, GT. WESTMINSTER HOUSE, LONDON, S.W

I don't know if I should tell you this, but my Dad killed the odd (occasional) sheep and we had mutton. We didn't even have electricity, so there was no fridge to keep the meat in, just a cold slab in the larder. So we got sick of the meat before we finished it.

We had an old-fashioned wireless at that time which run by battery. As the battery only lasted so long, the wireless was only allowed on for the news, *ITMA (It's That Man Again)* and Wilfred Pickles in *'Have a Go.'* Oh, and Dad like his boxing, so he'd listen to any boxing matches.

One day, we had a whole squadron or whatever of Americans turn up at the house. They had been on a route march and were supposed to meet their food-van at Kentmere, but got lost. These Americans were very polite and one came to the door and had this discussion with my dad about, "We don't want anything off you, just somewhere to sleep." But Dad milked a cow, and with the milk Mam made them a big pan of porridge. We had this huge, long, zinc hut where we kept all our machinery, sheep and bracken for animal bedding. So Dad let these soldiers go in there to sleep on the bracken. They stayed the night but were up and gone early next morning. Later Mam got a lovely letter from the bloke in charge of the Americans, thanking her and Dad for their help.

We had a man who came to do casual work on the farm. Us kids got

157

stopped going to school because we caught scabies off him. He used to have his meal with us and start scratching. Then we'd all start scratching and wondered what was wrong. Well, it was scabies and we couldn't go to school until we got rid of it. Everybody must have thought, "Oh, they're a dirty lot, getting scabies." It's like getting nits today if you're sitting next to somebody.

Longsleddale c.1940
Freda, centre, between her
older brother and sister

During the summer, at haytime we sometimes had eight to ten Italians helping. They came by bus from Bela Prisoner-of-War Camp at Milnthorpe. Because we were the last dropping off farm for prisoners, the bus driver stayed for the day. He never did any work, just slept in the bus.

These Italians brought their own sandwiches, or doorsteps as my mother used to call them. She used to feed these doorsteps to our horse. He liked those jam sandwiches, did our horse. Then she made a big basket of sandwiches up for these lads.

We had a prisoner, Babusca Sebastiano, come to live with us. But first somebody came to inspect his room and make sure that he'd be treat reasonably. I'll tell you what, when he settled in, us kids used to pinch his cigarettes. He'd obviously know we were pinching them because he only ever had a packet of ten. And none of us three kids really smoked. It was just something to do. Isn't it awful? Bless him, poor lad.

I remember coming home from school one day and my mother saying to me, "Keep away from Babusca tonight. He's upset." He'd had a letter from home saying that his mother had died. By the time he'd got the letter, she would have been buried. It was very sad.

I don't know much about the bomb that dropped on Cooper House, killing eleven people. I remember it being talked about but my mother would say, "It's nothing to do with you. You don't want to worry about that." You see, in them days, youngsters weren't told much and we were very naive.

When my sister used to say to me, "Babusca wants to go for a walk. You'll have to come with me because I'm not going with him on my own,"

Having a break at Longsleddale during haytime
L to R: ?, Harry Thistlethwaite, Geordy Willan, Billy Bland, Jack Bennett.
Foreground: Saverio (Italian POW)

I thought nothing about it and went as chaperone every time. Babusca was only with us for about six weeks but he wrote to my sister when he went back to Italy. I was sure it was about wanting to marry her. My mam's reaction was, "It's nothing to do with you, Freda. Keep your nose out of it." And it wasn't mentioned again.

The prisoners-of-war were still here in 1947. That was the year of the heavy snow and we were absolutely snowed up for six weeks. Nobody could get up to the top of the valley at all. So that was another job for the prisoners. They were brought up the valley and cut the snow out in blocks and threw them over the hedges. A road was opened to the school and the church by these men as the snowplough couldn't do it.

My mother used to sell the odd pound of butter here and there during the war. After the war she was in hospital and got friendly with a ward sister. Well, even though the war had finished, it was still difficult to get butter. So this sister used to come up to Longsleddale on a Saturday. My mother would sell her some butter, and away went the ward sister on the bus with her butter.

Well, when I was fifteen and left school, my mother wrote to the ward sister saying, "Freda's left school, is there any jobs going at the hospital?" And that's how I got my first job. Me going with my ration book to live in at the hospital and be a scullery maid, peeling spuds.

It wasn't until more than fifty years after the war, and my sister had been dead for some time, that my mother told me the story of Babusca. After he returned home to Italy, he wrote to my sister asking to marry her. He said that if she'd go to Bela Camp and collect a box belonging to him, inside was something for her. But she burnt the letter and never collected his belongings.

Freda was a scullery maid and then cook until marriage. Victor was a lorry driver until retirement. Now grandparents, both Freda and Victor are Vice Presidents of Kendal Cricket Club.

TWENTY THREE

'Always smiling. Always happy'

✍

Eleanor Tinkler, born 1900 at Hull. One of ten children, Eleanor's family came to Maryport in 1901 when her father was appointed Chief Customs Officer at the town port.

Eleanor today

In 1914, two of my brothers, Jim and Tom, went to war. The eldest one, Jim needn't have gone at all, because he was in the customs at Middlesbrough, a reserved occupation. The second brother, Tom, an engineer, he had joined the Yorkshire Territorials because he got a fortnight's free camp holiday. He was on holiday when the war broke out and returned to join the Yorkshire Regiment. So of course, Jim put down his pen and went with him.

They were in the first stages of that terrible war. The first year of 1914 was dreadful. Both brothers were in the front line. Jim got shot in the head and his eye was hanging over his cheek. Tom carried him on his back for two miles to the hospital. My mother got a telegram to go to the military hospital on the south coast where Jim had been sent. So she went down and stayed there for about six weeks, next-door to the hospital.

Jim lived. A noted surgeon had been doing work on my brother's face. The eye was out, so he put a lid over it. Then a channel was made down Jim's nose and a silver plate put in his head. "I think you'll do, Woodgate." said the surgeon. "What are you going to do with your one eye?" "Well sir," Jim answered, "I can see more than you can. I can see a surgeon with two eyes and you can only see a broken-down man with one eye." Very quick on the draw, very witty was my brother.

My second brother, Tom, had his leg blown off. His regiment were blowing up bridges to keep the Germans from following them. The Germans got in front of them and mined the bridge and that's where Tom got his leg blown off. He was put on the beach with other casualties and taken onto a hospital ship. Now, the hospital ship had two thousand wounded on board. Over the top of the ship and on the prow, a red cross was painted. The Germans bombed the ship out of the water.

A month later, a body was washed up on the coast of Holland. It had my brother Tom's tag on, with his number, regiment and everything. The person who found the body took the tag off and it was sent to the War Office, who returned it to Tom's wife. And that was that.

Then in the Second World War my own son Dennis went. He won the same naval scholarship as my third brother, to go to Commander Fry's Naval School on the south coast. He went when he was thirteen, did two years as a cadet, and then he was drafted into the regular service.

When Dennis was seventeen, and on board ship, it was attacked by the Italians. He and sixteen others were sent to Capetown, South Africa, because they were classed as junior cadet officers. The rest of the crew were drafted about.

Dennis went to New York to join his ship when it had been repaired. While he was there, he stayed with a Mrs Churchill and she used to write to me every week and say how they all loved my son. He really was bonny. Always smiling. Always happy.

I worried a lot about Dennis because we'd lost about sixteen ships coming over from America. But a boy who lived close by me and who was in the merchant navy on the same convoy rushed to see me. He said, "Oh, Mrs Tinkler, Dennis is on the last ship in the convoy. He'll be home in about four days' time. You can expect a telegram any time." Instead of that, I got a telegram saying he'd been killed. That really ... it really broke me.

I remember Dennis's last home leave. It was when the lights, little blue lights were dimmed on the railway stations. And on leaving me, it was the first time in all his leaves that he ever said, "Good-bye, Mum."

Now widowed, with a family, Eleanor still lives at Maryport.

TWENTY FOUR

'The King won't get you home'

cso

Eileen Williams, born at Staveley, near Kendal.

I was working at Kentmere Box Limited at Staveley, just sorting out the photographic paper in the darkroom when the war broke out. Everything continued as normal, except, of course, people were going into the army.

There were some troops stationed at Bowness-on-Windermere and some on Fellside at Kendal because my brother Jack, started off there. He was in the Territorials when war broke out and he went up Fellside to start with, before they moved on to help make the prisoner-of-war camp at Grisedale Hall.

That was the only thing you saw, people just disappearing sort of style, and that was it. Beyond that, no, you never thought much about war. Not until Jack was taken prisoner. He was in the commandos and was one of the unlucky ones who were caught at the raid on Saint Nazaire. I think that was really when war came home to people, you know. Then there was a young chap from the village, he was killed in France. It was them sort of things that really hit you. People weren't coming back.

When my brother was taken prisoner, we got a telegram from the War Office letting us know. We were able to send him letters but you always remembered that careless talk cost lives. So there wasn't a lot to write about but at least Jack was allowed to send us postcards from Germany. If my mother wanted to send a food parcel to Germany, she got in touch with the local branch of the Red Cross who dealt with parcels going to prisoner-of-war camps.

Dad was a woodcutter, but when war started he was in the fire service at Staveley. Later on he moved to Kendal fire station. Because of the shifts he did, he stayed with my auntie at Kendal. My other brother was wood felling until he went into the army. My youngest brother and sister were only at school.

To be honest, I don't think rationing made a lot of difference. You got your food just the same and also there wasn't a lot of different food like today. It was always just a bit of meat and vegetables. I don't like vegetables – never did, so I wasn't really interested in food. And we weren't always buying clothes before the war, so that didn't affect us. We used soap for washing our hair and then put curlers in our hair. When curlers were in short supply, I was down at Manchester and used to get someone to bring bits of electric wire to use instead, and put those in my hair. I know some women used to put gravy browning on their legs when they couldn't get stockings. But that would have been too much trouble for me.

I think I got a bit fed up at Kentmere Box and said I'd have a change. So I went to Short Brothers at Troutbeck Bridge as they were taking anybody on, whether you could do anything or not. Short Brothers came up to Windermere after the war started and built flying boats. It was quite a big place – a light, airy place with good buildings. There was also a building by the lake where they were supposed to be going to shunt these planes out. I only once went to a hangar by the lake edge. That was what we called the paint shop, and they were spraying with this celluloid stuff and the smell was terrible.

Short's was quite pleasant to work at, actually, and I had different jobs there. One was making little holes in struts. I finished up engraving the pieces that went in the cockpit of planes. That was a nice job, that was. I only ever saw one body of a plane. See, they made them in bits, what they called struts and fastened them on. The RAF used to come with the stuff we needed on a low loader, as the wings were ready made.

I can't remember my wage but you were paid by the time it took you to finish a job. So if you were well in with the person who did the time sheets, you would tell them to put you extra time on. You told the young chap, "I want more time for that". Then I got more money at the end of the week. It wasn't a place where people were pushed to work very hard. You were just given your bits of metal and told what to do with it. Nobody seemed to bother you a lot. We worked Saturday mornings, but even before the war,

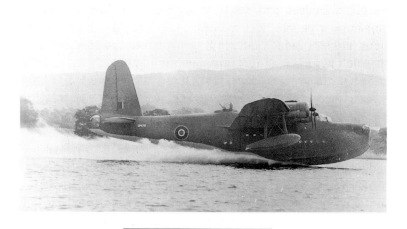

Short's Sunderland Mk II

folk worked on a Saturday.

Short's employed a lot of people. Most were locals but quite a number were brought up from the south, at Rochester where the company was based. First of all, they were in lodgings and then little cottages were built for the workers. These cottages weren't very elaborate, but they were somewhere for folk to live. After the war, quite a few of the workers from away stayed in the area. But the little bungalows were pulled down when they built the secondary school. People had to be rehoused who'd lived

there for years.

We had a canteen and a sort of Workers Playtime. Not entertainers coming in, just people who worked there. They'd get people up to do different 'turns'. I didn't bother a lot about food. So whether I got any or not, it didn't matter to me. But the canteen was a nice, big one and there was a lovely cloakroom. Probably far better than any other factories had. You see, in them days, not everybody had water closets at home. Well, at Shorts, the cloakroom was so spacious and beautifully tiled with washbasins and toilets.

I always remember I used to work with an elderly lady and when she wanted to work overtime, she'd say, "I'll buy you a Welsh rarebit for your tea if you'll stop with me." She wanted the extra money, so if I was that side out, I'd stop with her until about eight o'clock. That was the latest you could work but nobody forced you to work. But my aim was getting out of there. When I finished work, I was off.

There was nowhere really to go at nights in Staveley. They did start to bring pictures once a week to the village hall. That was all right and something to do. Some of us used to go to the Winter Gardens at

Eileen at Manchester

Morecambe. It cost one shilling and sixpence for the dance and one shilling for the train. We always had to run to catch the last train back home. One night at the end of the dance, my friend said, "I'm standing for the National Anthem." "Never mind about the damn Anthem, the King won't get you home," I told her. Well, we run for the train and just saw its tail lights disappearing. We had to stop on the station all night and catch the milk train back home, the next morning.

Towards the end of the war, the management at Shorts just came round and told quite a few of us, we were going to Manchester to work and that was it. You got no choice, you were just told to go. Your railway ticket was sent to you and off you went. There was about eight of us went from Staveley all together, so it wasn't so bad.

We went to the Ford Motor Company and my job was milling conrods for Lancaster bombers. When we were taken to the factory, we thought we were walking miles through this factory. The first place we came to had all these dark men working. Hundreds and hundreds of them and not a white face. We'd never seen so many dark people before and I suppose it was a shock at first. But we never bothered after that. They were workers same as us, whatever their colour or creed.

The first place we stayed at was the Co-operative Holiday Camp at a place called Culcheth, near Warrington. Oh, that was great. Just two in a room. There was a dance hall, shops and post offices on the site. Later on, we moved to a hostel nearer work. It was a total change for us. You see, you could get on a train and off you could pop to Manchester and spend weekends in Bellevue. We used to go to the motor-bike racing in the afternoon, then on to the fairground and finish up in the two big dance halls at night. That's where they used to bring the big bands. You know, Joe Loss and Geraldo. We thought it was great.

But it was down in Manchester that it really hit you there was a war on. You were always getting air raids and had to scuttle into the shelters. You see, at Staveley you could go up to what we called 'The Scar' and see the glow in the sky when they were bombing Barrow. That was about all we had, except for the time Selside was bombed.

Because we were down at Manchester, we were on a better wage. We'd never paid income tax on our wages and said we weren't going to pay any then. The chap in the wages office said it was for graduated pensions and asked me for the money I owed them. I said, "I'll tell you what. If I have to wait for my graduated pension, you wait for your share of income tax." And they did. I wasn't paying them any money. Oh, no.

Because we were from the country, we took a lot of stick about being country bumpkins. So we stood up for ourselves and demanded more money and told them what we wanted to do and not what they wanted us to do. Mind, there was some nice people there but our foreman wasn't so nice. Years later, I met him on the prom at Morecambe and I felt like knocking him into the sea and getting my own back.

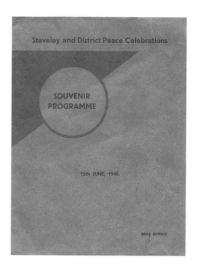

Staveley and District Peace Celebrations

SOUVENIR PROGRAMME

15th JUNE, 1946.

PRICE SIXPENCE

We were down at Manchester when the war finished. So it wasn't long before we were packed off home. We weren't that bothered about being pushed off because they were running down. A lot of the factories there were just made for the war effort and they closed them pretty rapidly after the war.

I was back at Staveley for VJ Day and got into trouble. I went with another woman into the Duke of Cumberland pub for a drink and my dad played hell. I was twenty-one years old, but women didn't go into pubs round here at that time.

Brother Jack, arriving home at Staveley from P.O.W. camp in Germany

Back home, I went to work at Cropper's Paper Mill at Burneside and it was quite nice there. You just went and asked for a job and got one. There was no problem with getting jobs in those days. It was at Burneside that I saw the Eyeties, (Italian POW's) because they were on farms round there. They used to roam about and always wanted to talk to you. I didn't bother about talking to them as there's good and bad in everybody. But I used to feel sorry about the food they brought from Bela (POW Camp). It was like dog biscuits, it was horrible. There was also some Germans as well as the Italians working at Staveley. Now, they weren't very nice and some were quite aggressive.

Brother Jack

I'd much preferred working at Manchester as there was more to do. I wasn't even interested in men. I hadn't time. I would rather have a good time and go out with the lassies. To the picture houses, Bellevue, even just a walk round all the shops. I suppose I came back because everybody else came back. We were all together. Or put it this way, like a lot of sheep. But it look a bit of getting used to, coming back. Things weren't just on hand, and we'd had freedom. Lovely freedom.

Eileen, who is now a widow, continued working at J. Cropper & Co. Ltd,
before returning to Staveley Wood Turning Co. Ltd
where she worked until marriage.

TWENTY FIVE

'Everybody's been in Latvia'

∽

Karlis Junga, born 1922 in Latvia.

I was born in the district of Cesis, in Latvia. Actually I was born in the middle of a wood, in a foresters house as my father was a farmer, forester and blacksmith. Our country has seen many wars and been invaded by Germans, Russians, Swedes and Poles. Everybody's been in Latvia.

In 1939, the Russians came in. You could do nothing about it. They just came in and that was that, like. When there was so many millions of Russians and just two million Latvians, you can do nothing about it.

Karlis

To start with, they just took a larl bit of land from our farm and left us with thirty hectares. Again, you can do nothing about it. Then in June 1940 they took about thirty-two thousand of our best people. The educated, the teachers and shopkeepers. They put them in cattle wagons, and away to Siberia. Thousands and thousands of people would just disappear. We were lucky as the Russians never took anybody away from our family.

171

One day in 1941 I saw my first Russians running away. And the Germans came and we celebrated until they took the Jews away. That was the biggest mistake they made. In Latvia we had plenty of Jews in towns and in every business.

Then I went to war against the Communists with the Latvian Army. Oh, it was bad. The wrong war for the wrong things. A hard life. We fought on the Eastern Front, then started to retreat and came back through our own country. All our divisions went to Poland and re-formed again. We had a good fight when the Russians came in there. Then I was wounded with shrapnel and sent to Denmark to convalesce.

From Denmark, I came back to the front again. In 1945 we went to meet the Yankee army. The other way, we would have been trapped by the Russians. We were transferred to a displaced persons' camp on the East coast of Germany. After that we were sent to a big Stage Three camp in Belgium. In 1946, we were sent back to Germany. I was at that camp for about three months and we had the opportunity to come to England for farm work or mines.

About one hundred and forty of us came to England. Maybe fifty percent Latvians. The others were Poles, Ukrainians, Czechs, Estonians,

Brougham Camp

and even the odd German. To tell the truth, I didn't know what England would be like. I couldn't even say 'Good morning' in English.

We landed at Hull and were taken to a transfer camp. The next morning we went into Hull with our money. You know, two pounds of sugar cost only fivepence. With a pound of sugar you can make whisky, just like that. And walking down the street in Hull, we see road-men working. In them

II - 148
J 139953

(1) REGISTRATION No.	A.E.F. D.P. REGISTRATION RECORD		For coding purposes
G2 1 9 1 7 2 0 9	Original ☑ Dublicate ☐		A. B. C. D. E. F. G. H. I. J.

		M. ☑ Single ☑ Married ☐	
JUNGA	KĀRLIS	F. ☐ Widowed ☐ Divorced ☐	LATVIAN
(2) Family Name	Other Given Names	(3) Sex (4) Marital Status	(5) Claimed Nationality

4.18./22 CĒSU PAG.	CĒSU APR.	LATVIA	EVANGELIC	(8) Number of Accompanying Family O
(6) Birthdate Birthplace	Province	Country	(7) Religion (Optional)	Members:

(9) Number of Dependents: O	JUNGA JĀNIS	EZERGAILIS EMILIJA
	(10) Full Name of Father	(11) Full Maiden Name of Mother

(12) DESIRED DESTINATION	(13) LAST PERMANENT RESIDENCE OR RESIDENCE JANUARY 1, 1938.
	DRABEŽU PAG. CĒSU APR. LATVIA

City or Village	Province	Country	City or Village	Province	Country
FARMER				TRACTOR-DRIVER	
(14) Usual Trade, Occupation or Profession	(15) Performed in What Kind of Establishment	(16) Other Trades or Occupations			

a. LATVIAN b.	c.	(18) Do You Claim to be a Prisoner of War	V		(19) Amount and Kind of Currency in your Possession
(17) Languages Spoken in Order of Fluency			Yes No		

(20) Signature of Registrant:	(21) Signature of Registrar:	Date: 23 5 46	Assembly Center No. 1226

(22) Destination or Reception Center: /						
	Name or Number	City or Village		Province		Country

(23) Code for Issue	1	2	3	4	5	6	7	8	9	10	11	12	13	14	15	16	17	18	19	20	21	22	23	24	25	26	27	28

(24) REMARKS

'Karlis' Registration Record'

days, there was a lot of workmen on the roads. Now, they all wore shirts of all colours, but without a collar. But every one of them wore a tie. To tell you the truth, it was the biggest laugh in my life. I didn't know why they put on a tie when they didn't have a collar.

From Hull we came up to Brougham Camp near Penrith. It was an old army camp but we had no trouble with it. Then I went to work on the farms. That was in 1946. It was the back end (Autumn) when we started work and it was all work by hand. Well, I was born and bred on a farm. I'm not worried about farm work.

The best farmer was Mr Hunter at Kirkby Thore. He was all right, like. All the money we earned went to the camp. But whenever I said, "Mr Hunter, you give me five shillings," I got five shillings.

We were working in England, but we all dreamed we would go back to Latvia and get our farms back and be back to normal. My mother and father had heard nothing of me from 1944 to 1948. By then the Russians were back in Latvia and took more of our farm land and we only had three acres left.

I reckoned it was about 1940 that I lost contact with my brother, Janis. He finished training school and was second Commander of a ship which went to Russia. Meanwhile war broke out and his ship was turned back to Leningrad. Janis had a bad throat and they took him off ship and put him

Brougham Camp c.1947
Karl standing centre

in hospital. And that's where he was stuck, in Leningrad. He went through all the siege of Leningrad.

After the war, Janis studied at university at Leningrad. He finished up a professor of engineering. He landed home to Latvia in roughly 1951 and is retired now. One sister has gone now. The other one who was six when I left, she'll be sixty next year. It's a long time, like. We have never met up again. But you never know, one day ...

Karlis, who still lives in Penrith was a farm worker
and council worker until he retirement.

TWENTY SIX

'*Wat a carryun!!*'

ᑫᑫᑎ

Maria Winters, nee Stewart, born 1920, at Gas Row, Cockermouth.

Me dad wus a Stewart. Aye, he wus a gypsy. He used tu be a reet 'Steptoe, un gar collectin rags. We hed a bit uf a fish business on a flat cart. Fish frae Lowestoft, et used tu cum on't train in a box. Et hev past five in't mornin, we used tu gar up't station un bring't fish doon yam. Theer wus neeah fridges or owt, so't fish wus put on ah stand ootsed t'back yat.

Me muther, she cud fillet fish und et wus cald in a mornin diuun ut. Thu used tu waarm yur finngers in ah basin uf hot watter. That wuz me job, fillin tu basin, see she cud put ur finngers in un tek't ice off thum. Tu fish wus aw put in greaseproof piapper un takken tu Lorton und Loweswatter on't hoss un cart. Ah hed tu put t'hoss in't shafts un put it's gear on un then wi went. Me dad, he used tu gar wid a white pinny on un ah used tu gar walkin wid him. See, we're talkin' aboot fowr miles theer un fowr miles back, eh? He waadn't let thu sit on't cart. Weel, that wus becos t'wuz owr much weight fur't hoss.

Dicky Pommer

Dad did fowr days a week on't business. On Thursday, he hed a day off. He waadn't gar nowheer on a Thursday. In thum days, a weef didn't gar oot tu wurk, unless they went un dun a bit ef wallpiaperin. That's wat mu muther did un charged hef-a-croon. Et wuz a livin, an existence, thet's aw. Un uf course, me faather drank like a lot uf men did.

Ah left St Joseph's School wen ah wuz fowrteen. Ah sed tu me mam, "Ah's gaaun oop tu Kezzick tu git a job tu help thu owt." Me twin bruther, Dickie went wid mu. We startid et t'pencil factury et Kezzick, sandpiaperin' on a machine. Ef thu'd sen t'size uf t'machine un here wuz us laal yans. Dickie wuz that laal, he hed tu stand on a box. Secund day et wurk, ah got under ah machine un cried. Weel, wid nivver beeun uway frae yam on oor own. Wat a carryun.

Yur hed t'wurk fur twelve munths at t'pencil factury ufoor yer got a rise ef a shillin'. But ah dun aw reet et Kezzick. Theer wuur vera, vera kind people theer. Ah wuz shifted five times un ended oop uz a pencil sorter. Yur nivver stuck et yan job. As yan persun left, yur stood on seniority tu move on. So ah'd probably end oop wid aboot eighteen shillin's un eleven punce a week.

By 1939, Dickie un me wuz still at t'pencil factory. Jake, oor eldest bruther wuz diunn quarry wurk un Billy un John wurked on t'faarms et Kezzick. Leon, tu youngest wuz still et school. Than Muther startid gittun unweel un poor soul, fur aboot three munths she laid in bed. T'auld doctor cum un diagnosed cancer un cudn't diuu nowt. So uz weel as mu own wurk, ah hed tu wesh fur t'five lads un mu faather in a big old fashioned dolly-tub thet wuz in't wesh-hoose. We hed neeah leets or candles. Theer wuz neeah oilcloth, ivverything wuz just bare boards un ah hed tu scrub wid Jeyes Fluid. When ah'd dun thet, ah'd tu keep mu faather garn wid his fish business. Gut the fish, like. So yur wur diuun ivverything on t'back-kitchen tiable in yan laal bit uf a hoose. Ah sumtimes think back un say, 'Weel, hoo did yur manage?" Becos yur hed tu cook un diuu. Like, yur hed yur oven but yur put t'fire on fust, tu git it garn. Un aw't time, mu muther waad be lyin' oop-stiaars. Tu safeguard us kids, mu muther wrote tu t'fish-merchunt un telt him nut tu hold us responsible fur any debts. Et really wuz a hard life fur mu muther. Ah wuz just beginnin tu larn mare aboot ur, like, when she deed. Mu muther wuz Belgian un off gentry folk. She'd beeun educated in a convent et Bruge in Belgium un cum ovver here uz a refugee in't Furst Wurld Waar.

But mu muther nivver went back tu Belgium uz she got pregnant un wuzn't married. Yur see, Cockermooth Wurk Hoose wuz on't gar et that time un wen lassies hed babbies ufoor they wuz wed, they used tu put them in theer. Efter me muther left the Wurk Hoose un married mu dad, t'laal lad she hed deed. His neet shut cawt fire wid a candle un he wuz burnt tu deeth. She'd luved that lad. She used tu sit un cry fur hoors on end because she wuz a lonely wumun.

Me boss at pencil mills, Mr Yates, wuz a real nice fella. Ah telt him aboot yam. He sed tu me, "Maria, Ah'm givin' yur a shillin' extra if yur'll clean me office oot fur me. Un Ah'm ganna encourage yur tu join this insurance scheme that'll give yur a bit extra if yur off badly." Wi called that oor badly money. So ah got t'job ef cleanin' t'office. Ah diunn aw this bass mattin'. Ah hed tu pick aw these mats oop un scop them oot thu window ufoor ah startid cleanin'.

Oor Billy un John got hired fur six munths et a time wid faarm wurk un didn't git paid until theer time wuz oop. So ah hed that tu contend wid. Ah wuz givin' them a shillin a week oot uf mu wage un hed aw theer weshin' tu bring doon frae Kezzick. We're tawkin aboot corderoy pants un aw farm clares. Ah hed tu wesh aw thet in't wesh hoose on a Saturday. We hed a passage un ah used tu hang claares oop tu dry. Then on't Monday, ah'd tek theer weshin' wid

ISSUED BY THE MINISTRY OF FUEL AND POWER

GAS and ELECTRICITY

WARNING

Ice-bound coal trains and road transport, an unprecedented strain on gas works and power stations — these were the consequences of the recent abnormal weather. It will take time for coal stocks to recover from the effects of these conditions.

All consumers must make a special effort to cut down their consumption of gas and electricity at home and in the works, in offices, in shops, restaurants and hotels. This must be done not, only in the interests of economy but in order to enable stocks to be built up again as rapidly as possible.

From industry an all-round cut of 10% has been asked. Maximum economies must be made in domestic consumption. The increase in domestic demand has been marked even in areas which have suffered little or no bomb damage.

ONLY THE MOST DRASTIC ECONOMY WILL ENABLE WAR PRODUCTION TO BE CARRIED ON AT FULL PRESSURE.

me tu t'pencil mills un et dinner-time, trail right oop tu't farms wuur they wuz wurkin.

Noo me dad wuz a reet, kind old fella. His nickname wuz Dickie Pommie. Ivverybody liked him. But he cudn't cope. He startid actin' oop un he lost his fish business. When he wuz thet way owt wid drink, he'd put us oot, lock, stock un barrel. We wuur put oot fur nowt. Ah'd cleaned un scrubbed fur him un kept us clean but he still put us oot. A policemun cum un asked neighbours in't street if they'd tek us in. Me eldest bruther cud luck efter his-sell. John un Billy lived-in on't farms. Dickie got lodgings, then went oop tu Scotland tu wark un joined t'Royal Artillery. So we're tawkin aboot keepin' oor Leon oot of a yam.

Anyway, this wummun frae Gas Row, she sed she'd tek me un Leon in.

177

She hed less room than we hed at yam becos she hed a big family. Ah paid ur twelve shillins fur me keep un six shillins fur Leon's keep. That wus eighteen shillins un wus neeah good tu me uz ah hed neeah munny left. Ah hed tu cum back tu Cockermooth un fiind wurk theer. Ah got a job et Miller's Shoe Factory.

Et Miller's, they startid me off un a big wheel, a big press. Ah put soles on't slippers. Ah pulled doon this clamp un et blew sixty punds uf pressure on't slippers. So yer wurked hard tu keep thum slippers movin' un hadn't tu stop. Yer hed neeah breaks un just tuk a sandwich wid yer tu wurk. Me startin wage wus twenty-five shillins un ah startid et eight in't mornin' un finished et hafe-past-five at neet. Like, wid young lads gaarn ter waar, yer hed tu tek mens' jobs.

Ah kept garn et Miller's un mekin me wages oop until ah got up tu aboot thirty-five shillins a week. Noo then, et got a bit easier fur me wen I wuz doon et Millers. So ah did a bit ef wurk fur t'Wummuns' Voluntary Service, meetin t'evacuees frae't trains un tekin' thum tu whear they wuur stayin. An ah weshed t'steps uf t'Catholic Chuuch un polished aw't candles un brasses.

Ah moved into a hoose wid Leon un shared it wid annnuther wumun. So thet meant when ah cum back frae wurk, ah wurked un scrubbed theer uz weel. Me bruther slept on an old sofa un ah slept in a bed. He wuz still only a bit ef a kid, un menny a time ah felt like gettin hum off t'sofa un tuckin hum in back uf mu.

Sumbody ah knew, left theer laal babby wid mu. Noo then, ah hadn't a clue wat tu diuu wid't laal lass uz ah wuz wurkin aw day. She wuzzent a yaar old un on condensed milk un Farley's rusks. Ivverything hed tu be kept clean un dry but t'laal lass, she nivver tuk any harm wid me.

Theer wuz an old wumun lived in t'siaam yard et back uf us un she kept an eye on ur. Un wen ah think wat ah did – really, ah wuz diuun wrang leavin' her – yur waadn't dare do it tuday. But yur did it, then. Theer wusn't aw this rigmarole like theer is tuday.

A policemun cum tu Miller's lucken fer me. Ah wuz flait tu deeath uf policemun. Yur daren't hev a policemun ower yur yat-step. He sez, "Isst tha lucken efter a laal lass? Yur'd better cum yam wid me cos we're tekkin ur uway till a yam." Weel, ah telt hum that he'd better git in touch wid t'muther. They did manage tu finnd ur un she cum back. So t'babby wazzent tekken uway. Weel, wid aw this, un strugglin' aw't time, ah got a bad chest un TB wuz suspected. Me faather got tu know aboot aw this un went mad un sed, "Yur'll cum back yam."

Ah went back yam un wuz ef wurk wid me bad chest, so ah went wid t'gypsies campin. We went oop tu Appleby Fair. Oh, et wuz aw reet. I wuz wid me aunt,old Jane McGee frae Wigton. Now, she wuz a reet gypsy un she wuz a kind old wumun. We went in't covered wagons as theer wuz neeah fancy trailers et that time. Aunt Jane went in a combination. That's a flat cart, wid wooden hoops un a watter-proof sheet ower et.

It used tu tek us three days tu gar oop frae Cockermuth tu Appleby. We aw used tu sleep in't covered wagons. On't way, mebbe et farms et Lorton or Buttermere, we'd buy hafe a sheep un chickens. Tu chickens wud be cooked, put in a big wooden box un they'd last uz nearly a full week. That wuz becos thur wuz neeah uvens in't wagons un yur cooked owwer t'old camp fire.

Efter that week, ah went back yam but ah didn't stay theer vera lang. Ah rented a laal hoos in't next yard. It hed a livin room wid a fire-place un a

Maria. C. 1942

laal cooker. Upstairs wuz yan bedroom un an attic room. Toilet un wesh-hoos wuz ootside. Fust thing ah got wuz sum oilcloth squares tu put on't top of t'stiane flags. Then ah went tu t'auction un bowt an iron bed fur messel un a couch fur me bruther, Leon. Then ah got two straw mattresses fur me uther bruthers or any of theer mates wen they cum frae t'waar. That wuz so they cud stay a couple of neets un sleep on't shakey downs. Ah'd prommist me muther ah'd luk efter me bruthers un ah did. Ah did mu job.

But we nivver went hungry during t'waar. Fellas that used tu wurk ut slaughter hoose, they'd bring thoo a leg o' mutton un say, "Here, git that in t'oven." They did poach in them days, did thum lads. They aw did it.

We hed a Welcum Yam Fund in Gas Row fur't troops. Two old ladies used tu cum roond collectin' fur et. Than wen't lads cum yam on leave, they'd give thum this welcum yam munny. Un wen et wus cummin' on tu Christmus, yur'd knit gloves fur't lads still uway. Than git a copy of't Cumberland Star un put a letter inside et fur't lads tu read.

Oh, theer wus a lot of dances. Meybe aboot a shillin' tu git in. There wus dances in't Public Hall, Appletree Hotel un't Drill Hall. Soldiers wud cum doon frae't Wurk Hoose where they wuur billeted un Billy Bowman's band wud be playin'. Hoo t'lads kept t'roof frae cummin doon wid dancin' in theer boots, ah divn't know.

Ah met oop wid Ted me husband in 1944. Ted, he's a Dearham lad un wus in't regular army aw his leef until he wuz invalided oot. We got married in January 1944. Ah wore a wine coloured costume thet ah think Ted wud buy wid his discharge munny. Ah know that sum cakes fer't weddin' wuz med wid liquid paraffin becos yer cudn't git butter.

Me daughter, Octavia wuz born in November 1944. Ah used tu git white floor bags frae't floor mill. Ah'd steep thum in't old weshin boiler un thum dun fur nappies. Yur med yer own nappies in thum days. Oor district nuurse wud biake me bread un bring me oranges in exchange fur me clares coopons. Yur got cod liver oil frae't clinic but yur paid ten-un-a-hafe-pence fur national tinned milk. Menny a time ah hed neeah munny fur that. Ah'd ask me faather if ah cud borrer munny. But usually, yur daren't borrer owt. Yur couldn't pay it back. It wuz hard gaaun aw thu time tryin' tu mek ends meet.

By that time thu waar wuz owwer. Ah hed neeah luv fur't Germans then un ah still heven't. They wuur killin' oor lads. The Japanese waar wus still on. Ted, he'd bin in Burma but thu Japanese waar, yer nivver heerd et mentioned. That wuz thu forgotten waar. It waz a hard waar. Un it wus hard gaaun tryin' tu mek ends meet back here.

Nut lang ugar, I hed Australian television here tu see me. They wuur diuun a programme aboot kids that wur sent frae Yams tu Australia. Yur see, this is whaat they cum un askt me. "Hoo did ah manage tu keep me bruther oot of a Yam?" Weel, ah hed tu gar un wurk tu diuu it. Wurk, that's hoo ah did it. That kept me garin'. Un ah've allus dun charity wurk. Wurk ef sum kind, that's bin me leef.

Maria joining in the fun at
Cockermouth Carnival

Maria is married with one daughter and still an active charity worker.

TWENTY SEVEN

'It was all bed and work'

William Hornby, born in 1919 at Whitbeck.

I left school at fourteen. For a start off I stayed at home and then my dad said, "It's about time you were getting some work." I had a brother-in-law who worked in a slate quarry at Kentmere, so I went there.

When the quarry closed down I went to Staveley Wood Turning Company for fifteen shillings a week. I lived with an aunt at Staveley and paid her ten shillings. Then half-a-crown was for my insurance stamp and the rest was for me. My auntie couldn't feed me and do my washing and everything for ten shillings, so my dad said, "Get yourself back home." So back home I went, was on the dole for a bit, and then decided to go into farm work.

Well, I'm the youngest of nine and had a nephew who was the same age as me. He had a farm at Silecroft and I went and worked for him. That's when the war started. Everybody had seemed to think there'd be a war. It had been shaping that way, with Hitler the way he was.

GERMAN PARACHUTIST

LUFTWAFFE BADGE WORN ON RIGHT BREAST

GREY-GREEN OR CAMOUFLAGED GABERDINE OVERALLS ALWAYS WORN OVER TUNIC ZIP FASTENERS

PISTOL

GAUNTLET GLOVES DRAWN IN AT WRIST

BOMB POCKETS

LOOSE TROUSERS (Air Force Blue)

JACK BOOTS LACED AT SIDES HEAVY RUBBER SOLES

THIS BADGE ON RIGHT SIDE OF HELMET (EAGLE BADGE ON LEFT SIDE)

STEEL HELMET (CRASH HELMET SHAPE) WITH 2 CHIN STRAPS (May be camouflaged)

BINOCULARS

ROLLED CAPE

2 HAVERSACKS

WATER BOTTLE

DETAIL OF TUNIC

TUNIC (Air Force blue) PIPED SHOULDER STRAPS & COLLAR

UNIT NUMBER OF WHITE METAL

Parachute troops, both officers and men, are easily distinguished. Look for these features:—grey drill overalls and steel helmet with double chin strap and very small brim—like a motor cyclist's crash helmet. Lace-up boots with rubber soles. Heavy belts and cross straps, large pockets over thighs. If you're close enough, you'll see on his helmet and right breast a curved-winged eagle carrying a swastika. Remember he'll be in overalls. There's no khaki in a German uniform.

Anyway, the week after war started I was sent to Workington for my medical. I passed it A1 which I was pleased about. I've got a bit of a high arch on my foot and three different doctors had to pass me. I was never called up and I've always regretted it, really. Most of my mates were in the army, but that's the way it was.

Us farm lads who weren't in the army felt that we weren't doing anything to help until we joined the Home Guard. I joined at Silecroft and got a uniform and a Browning automatic gun. I never had any ammunition for the gun. I don't think anybody else had, unless they were the 'higher up's'.

In the Home Guard we met one night a week at the Mechanics Hall at Silecroft, from about half six or seven till nine o'clock at night. A chap who was an ex-sergeant major in the army trained us lot. And he did put us through it. We had drill, running, unarmed combat, cleaning and reassemble of guns. We were all frightened of this bloke. He was a terror. No messing with him.

Occasionally we did night duty, and I dozed off one night. The next thing I knew, my mate Bill was shaking me, saying, "Hey, Bill, they're (the Germans) coming. They're coming across the shiller.' Do you know what it was? It was all the rabbits going across the shiller to lick the sea salt.

My nephew moved to Holmrook and I went with him and joined the Drigg Home Guard. You can look back now and say the Home Guard was a waste of time but we enjoyed it. The great coat we were given, I used to

29

NUMBER of LIVESTOCK as returned the years 1939–44.

LIVESTOCK (number)   CUMBERLAND

	3rd June, 1939	4th June, 1940	4th June, 1941	4th June, 1942	4th June, 1943	3rd June, 1944
Cows and Heifers in milk	49,763	50,429	52,385	53,641	55,284	56,014
Cows in calf but not in milk	9,589	9,364	9,866	11,825	14,212	15,373
Heifers in calf with first calf	13,423	12,855	13,681	18,142	17,975	30,394
Bulls for service	2,684	2,622	2,707	2,964	3,077	3,225
Bulls (including Bull Calves) being reared for service	2,547	2,380	3,315	3,620	3,548	3,381
Other Cattle:—						
Two years and over { Male	34,375	13,533	16,204	11,108	10,282	9,677
‎ { Female		21,089	14,043	14,475	15,274	17,349
One year and under two { Male	49,868	10,144	15,414	12,018	10,341	9,592
‎ { Female		26,839	25,440	25,090	27,336	29,659
Under one year { Male	46,246	45,763	44,177	15,121	10,382	12,181
‎ { Female				31,377	33,415	33,370
TOTAL CATTLE and CALVES	199,496	201,328	191,232	201,181	201,630	210,383
Sheep over one year:—						
Rams for service	8,652	8,173	6,942	6,872	6,880	6,509
Ewes for breeding	278,218	206,867	230,165	227,926	280,949	205,200
Two-tooth (Shearling) Ewes	75,240	60,158	59,050	55,200	54,400	53,402
Others	47,344	57,801	69,213	53,109	50,679	48,485
Sheep under one year:—						
Ram Lambs intended for service	5,319	2,591	1,953	2,604	1,947	2,386
Others	334,749	308,351	253,560	252,257	215,088	214,383
TOTAL SHEEP and LAMBS	749,622	112,912	629,893	597,563	529,293	540,323
Sows in pig		1,496	633	694	545	469
Gilts in pig	2,766	625	224	544	309	221
Other Sows for breeding		725	545	545	491	439
Barren Sows for fattening		182	186	120	120	92
Boars for service	196	154	108	115	100	94
All Other Pigs:—						
Over five months	3,770	2,906	3,407	3,026	3,806	2,969
Two to five months	9,579	10,571	7,318	6,080	6,640	4,314
Under two months	5,716	4,802	2,929	2,990	3,291	2,411
TOTAL PIGS	21,627	21,561	15,362	13,061	14,372	11,099
Fowls over six months	475,677	508,050	496,225	365,121	318,003	301,437
Fowls under six months	609,492	463,296	291,615	338,103	279,521	333,627
Total Fowls	(1,076,169)	(971,306)	(777,840)	(607,224)	(597,614)	(635,064)
Ducks	32,234	31,306	23,709	25,452	24,728	28,952
Geese	24,525	23,987	21,706	21,076	20,570	20,197
Turkeys	21,215	18,031	12,358	10,716	10,529	11,274
TOTAL POULTRY	1,154,133	1,044,750	835,613	764,479	653,017	695,487
Horses used for agricultural purposes (including mares kept for breeding)	11,605	11,321	11,857	10,419	11,499	11,121
Unbroken Horses over one year	3,551	3,721	3,565	3,296	2,886	2,938
Light Horses under one year	228	180	122	124	26	139
Heavy Horses under one year	1,240	1,395	1,334	1,762	1,246	1,208
Stallions for service	131	117	103	92	89	116
All Other Horses	1,892	1,374	1,423	2,649	1,465	1,415
TOTAL HORSES	18,447	18,108	18,404	17,921	17,280	16,907

TABLE 2 *(continued).*—ACREAGE under CROPS and GRASS and in June in each of

CUMBERLAND

CROPS and GRASS (acres)

	3rd June, 1939	4th June, 1940	4th June, 1941	4th June, 1942	4th June, 1943	3rd June, 1944
Wheat	331	2,355	6,504	9,381	19,654	14,444
Barley	357	976	1,495	2,399	4,940	5,487
Oats	43,110	63,096	75,391	83,931	83,126	82,802
Mixed Corn	517	3,635	9,985	9,422	6,514	4,704
Rye for threshing	16	67	93	144	724	430
Rye for green fodder	}			{	26	7
Beans for stockfeeding	10	135	471	391	265	271
Peas for stockfeeding	2	11	55	139	137	104
Potatoes, first earlies	566	440	609	978	1,101	1,181
Potatoes, main crop and second earlies	4,446	6,324	11,012	13,718	14,148	13,400
Turnips and Swedes for stockfeeding (a)	18,806	15,002	19,547	20,502	21,749	22,891
Mangolds	1,752	2,053	2,092	1,978	1,608	1,277
Sugar Beet	24	29	34	155	119	108
Rape (or Cole)	780	665	1,229	1,641	2,084	3,241
Cabbage, Kale, Savoys, and Kohl Rabi, for fodder	568	980	2,066	2,047	2,025	2,098
Vetches or Tares	1	24	58	20	37	51
Lucerne (b)	—	—	1	2	—	—
Mustard for seed						15
Mustard for fodder or ploughing in	15	12	4	33	3	39
Flax for fibre or linseed	1	17	79	80	40	
Hops						
Orchards with crops, fallow or grass below the trees	260	275	316	275	271	243
Orchards with small fruit below the trees (see also p. 166)	42	48	29	34	24	30
Small fruit not under orchard trees (see also p. 166)	108	109	65	45	34	37
Vegetables (excluding potatoes) grown in the open (see also pp. 144 to 155)	391	527	637	602	709	935
Flowers grown in the open } (see also	92	56	48	23	17	17
Crops under glass } pp. 156 to 161)	13	10	16	13	14	19
All Other Crops	154	130	287	384	496	320
Bare Fallow	371	197	154	169	419	629
TOTAL ACREAGE of CROPS and FALLOW (TILLAGE)	69,555	97,783	130,872	148,974	160,519	155,972
Clover and Rotation Grasses for hay	45,242	48,135	47,177	50,829	58,841	59,363
Clover and Rotation Grasses for grazing	50,427	45,113	41,302	40,338	44,326	57,856
Total Clover and Rotation Grasses	(95,669)	(93,248)	(88,479)	(91,366)	(103,667)	(117,119)
TOTAL ARABLE LAND	165,224	180,031	219,351	240,140	263,586	272,191
Permanent Grass for hay	85,883	80,031	70,977	60,826	62,142	46,917
Permanent Grass for grazing	255,277	228,140	200,234	186,485	197,364	163,074
Total Permanent Grass	(341,160)	(308,241)	(271,211)	(247,288)	(259,506)	(209,991)
TOTAL ACREAGE of CROPS and GRASS (excluding Rough Grazings)	506,364	497,372	490,562	487,428	483,592	482,182
Rough Grazings—Sole rights	240,142	248,407	257,488	260,201	263,517	262,952
Rough Grazings—Common	102,022	101,906	101,905	101,905	102,002	100,970
TOTAL ROUGH GRAZINGS	342,464	350,312	359,393	362,106	365,519	363,922

	1939	1940	1941	1942	1943	1944
TOTAL AREA of CUMBERLAND (excluding Water)			961,554			

(a) In 1939 and 1940 includes Turnips and Swedes for human consumption.
(b) In 1943 and 1944 Lucerne was returned under Clover and Rotation Grasses.

183

wear it for working on the tractor. One day it was hot, so I shoved this coat on the back of the tractor. After a bit I could smell burning and it was the coat. It had fallen down over the exhaust and caught fire.

I only worked for my nephew a short time at Holmrook and then went to work for Mr Bateman at Thornbank Farm, near Gosforth. Those were the happiest days of my working life. I tell you, the time I worked there, I put on nearly two stone in weight. We used to have porridge for breakfast, and bread and cheese. Come nine o'clock, at drinking time, there was two thick slices of bread, a lump of cheese and a pot of coffee. At dinner time was a real good meal. It was a knife-and-fork do, then a pudding after that. At tea-time there was bread and cheese again. Come supper time, it was either boiled or scrambled eggs.

You see, I really had no home, with my mother dying when I was young. My eldest sister brought me up, and she had five kiddies of her own. Then my dad died at the beginning of the war. I never had a real home, like. So Bateman's farm was the next best thing.

Besides me, there was an old man who was seventy-three working for Mr Bateman. Willy Steele, he was called, and had only worked on two farms since leaving school at fourteen. He had a sister lived at Gosforth, and every Saturday night he'd take his washing to her. On a Thursday, Mr Bateman's son would take him to the post office to collect his pension. Willy would put most of his money in the bank and keep enough to buy himself an ounce of tobacco.

Oh heck, I don't know what my wage was, but I did all right. I know I didn't make five pounds a week, but I always seemed to have plenty of money and even opened a bank account. By the end of the war I had two hundred pounds saved up, which was a lot of money.

We had Ayreshire-cross cattle on the farm, that John Bateman used to buy at some place in Scotland. The milk was sent by Sharpe's wagons to Libby's at Milnthorpe. Libby's made a lot of farmers. If it hadn't been for them many farmers would have been bankrupt without the cheque coming in every month for milk.

When it was a busy time on the farm, we used to have the land girls. These girls lived at Bolton Hall, a big hostel at Gosforth. From there they were taken to the different farms to work. There was one little girl who used to come to the farm and oh, she was a beauty. She was spreading manure this particular time, and I went to have a word with her and saw that she was crying. She showed me her hands and they were red raw. I said, "You go and sit down behind that dyke. I'll scale this manure and tell Mr Bateman about your hands when I see him." Well, I saw Mr Bateman and he took her back to the farm, bandaged her hands up and got her to a doctor. Poor lass, she'd been a doctor's receptionist before joining the land army.

Oh yes, old Mr Bateman, he used to be bloody good to them lasses. He used to say, "When are you lasses going home to see your mothers? Come and see me when you're going and you can have some eggs." Well, he kept about a hundred ducks and would give them lasses a dozen eggs when they were going home. Then when they were working on the farm, he'd give them cigarettes to keep them going.

In them days you never thought about getting Saturday afternoon or weekends off. It was all bed and work, and you'd always been used to it. Mind, a bloke used to run the land girls to Egremont and he'd take us lads along. We went to the pictures on a Saturday night or to the dances at the Public Hall at Gosforth.

There used to be ENSA concerts at Millom every Saturday night. But they wouldn't let us farm lads in as it was only for troops. "Fair enough as we're only farm workers," I said, "but if we don't work, there's no food for the troops." Anyway, it was altered and we could go into the concerts. What were they like? Well you know, a laugh and a song.

If we went to Millom on a Saturday night and missed the bus back, we used to set off and run. We'd take a short cut and try and catch the bus as it went round Haverigg. Never made it in time, though. We'd be about a hundred yards away when the old bus would disappear round the corner, so we had to walk. I never wore a vest nor underpants in them days. I'd go to a dance or concert, walk back to the farm, and it would be freezing like hell all the way. I'd jump into bed and think nothing of it. But you were hard then. I wouldn't like to do it now.

As I say, good as Mr Bateman was, I didn't like to ask for an afternoon off. But one Thursday afternoon I came down to Ulverston on the train. The hirings were still running in the war years and when you got off the train, you couldn't get past these farmers. It was all, "Isn't thou for hire?" or "What dost thou do?" That was one thing, I was about thirty years on farming and I was never hired at a market.

We used to see the air-force lads arriving at Millom on their way to Haverigg for so many weeks training. First of all, the previous batch would leave and it was all tears with some of the women. Then the next night the new lads would arrive. It was an education to watch some of these women, the same ones who'd been crying the night before. Some of these women were all for uniform, and there was more of these women married than there was single ones. They had no eyes for the ordinary lads.

A few planes came down, but one in particular, it had a forced landing. We were harvesting in a field and this plane (Fairy Fulma) came over and landed in the next one. It was a top secret. A lot of airmen were billeted at farms roundabout, who took this plane to bits and took it away. It was nothing to do with Haverigg. I think it was the Fleet Air Arm.

The planes at Haverigg, they were used for training. Sometimes they'd tow targets for gun practice. But sometimes they used to release these targets too soon. Later, local kids would go and take the targets back to the air base and would get five shillings for doing it. Half the target was like netting or curtain stuff, only stronger. And the other bit was like canvas. Nearly all the farmers managed to get these every now and again for under their binders on a tractor.

I remember working in the field picking turnips one day, and this Lysander came over. It was hitting the ground and bouncing along. It hit the ground and went right over me. At the bottom of the field the plane caught a net fence with barbed-wire posts and pulled the lot out of the ground. So I think if it had caught me or the horse I was with, we'd both have been finished.

The ironworks were still on the go at Millom at that time. There'd been an air raid one night (2 January 1941) and one of the planes came over. It circled round and round, then dropped his load. A whole row of houses (Steel Green) went that night with a lot of people killed.

There was the gunnery ranges up at Eskmeals but we never knew what was going on there, even though I had a brother-in-law working there. When I lived at home before the war started, we used to see long railway wagons carrying sixteen inch guns that were being taken up to Eskmeals. All you ever knew was that guns were being fired, as you could hear the 'boom, boom' from them.

I used to go ferreting for rabbits at Whitbeck. Every Friday the big WD (War Department) wagons went up that way. Well, it didn't matter how many rabbits I caught, as these WD drivers always bought them off me for ten shillings a pair. That was good money, as the chap who used to buy them off me at Silecroft only used to pay one shilling and six pence or two shillings.

Do you know, I can't remember the local bobby ever coming to Bateman's farm. I suppose it was because they had no sheep. He used to go round the farms where there was sheep to make sure that the sheep dipping was done proper. So the only time I came in contact with the bobby was, when he caught me and some others playing nap (card game) on the war memorial steps one Sunday. Somebody must have reported us.

Come Christmas, and all the land-army girls had a Christmas party at Bolton Hall and we had a good time. There was one of the girls from Newcastle and I was taking her out. I was even thinking about going to Newcastle to meet her parents. Then I met Dorothy, who I married. Well, what a time that was, telling this Newcastle lass. If you were out anywhere, there she'd be crying away.

William at Egremont C. 1945

I don't remember VE Day but on VJ Day we were picking potatoes. Up came Mr Bateman with a drink and said, "Well now, when you've had this drink, you can all go home. It's the VJ celebrations from now until the weekend." I don't think I was sober after that. I don't think anybody else can have been, because we'd got about half a ton of potatoes up and nobody came for them and they wasted.

After that I moved down to Beetham to work on a farm, as I was marrying Dorothy and living down this way. That was the first time I ever got a five-pound note in my wage. Even though the war had finished, there was prisoners-of-war and displaced persons working on the farms. Good workers they were, too. Then came the bad winter of '47, when you were getting out of bed onto bare oilcloth and snow was half-way up the window-sill.

I met some nice folk through the war. I liked Gosforth and made good friends over that way. Looking back, the best working time of my life was at Mr Bateman's during the war years.

William, a married man with a family, was a farmer worker,
then council worker before retirement.

Index

191